6

IT Kids

FOUNDATION® BOOKS

RiiiT FUTURE UNLIMITED

Published by
Cambridge University Press India Pvt. Ltd.
under the Foundation Books imprint
Cambridge House, 4381/4 Ansari Road, Daryaganj, **New Delhi** 110 002

Cambridge University Press India Pvt. Ltd.
C-22, C-Block, Brigade M.M., K.R.Road, Jayanagar, **Bangalore** 560 070
Plot No. 80, Service Industries, Shirvane, Sector-1 Nerul, **Navi Mumbai** 400 706
10, Raja Subodh Mullick Square, 2nd Floor, **Kolkata** 700 013
21/1 (New No. 49), 1st Floor, Model School Road, Thousand Lights, **Chennai** 600 006
House No. 3-5-874/6/4, (Near Apollo Hospital), Hyderguda, **Hyderabad** 500 029
Agarwal Pride, 'A' Wing, 1308, Kasba Peth, Near Surya Hospital, **Pune** 411 011

IT Kids

First published 2007
Reprinted 2009 (Twice)

Content & Instructional design by:
Ms. Urmeela, V.
Mr. Srinath, S.
Ms. Laxmi Arun
Ms. Pavithra, M.

ISBN 978-81-7596-516-4

Registered Office:
Raman Computers Pvt. Ltd.
II Floor, Ballal Complex, Ashoka Circle,
K.M. Puram, Mysore-570005

Published by Manas Saikia for Cambridge University Press India Pvt. Ltd. and printed at Print Shop Pvt. Ltd., Chennai.

FOREWORD

RiiiT's *IT Kids* has an innovative approach to disseminate ICT in schools. Interactive method is used, focusing on concept-based learning with illustrations. In place of the conventional black-board system, which is teacher-centric, these materials create a student-centric environment where e-learning becomes effortless. Tips provided to students help them understand the concepts easily. *IT Kids* has been written in a non-technical style that the students are bound to find empowered and more informative.

This series present ICT as a tool and not as any other subject, facilitating full exploration of the potential of ICT. The curriculum introduces concepts appropriately in each level with suitable gradation and is consolidated by the time students pass out of 10th Standard. The IT Curriculum emphasises on "experiential learning" followed by reflection, discussion, analysis and evaluation of the experience.

Success of educational process depends on the quality, commitment and expertise of the teacher. To support teachers, **RiiiT** has taken many initiatives to provide quality resources to keep them abreast of the technology. The teacher's resource material has lessons to support class-wise contents and assessment methodology to implement the curriculum effectively. **RiiiT**'s *IT Kids* would definitely shape the future of IT Education in schools.

Dr. K Balaveera Reddy
Vice Chancellor
Visvesvaraya Technological University, Belgaum
December 23, 2005

TABLE OF CONTENTS

RECAP

Learning Objective: To revise the basics of MS Word, MS Excel and MS PowerPoint.

Overview of Word Processor

- MS WORD is a program present in MS OFFICE package.
- Word Processor is a software package that enables you to create, edit, print and save a document.
- Some of the important components of MS Word are Title Bar, Toolbar, Ruler, Status bar, Scroll bar, Work space, Main menu.

File Manipulations

You will learn to create, save and open an existing document in MS Word.

A page header is a text that is added to the top margin of every page. It can be a title of a document or a page number. A page footer is a text that is added to the bottom. Some of the functions are described as follows:

Shortcut Commands

Function	Shortcut command	Menus
Create a new document	Ctrl+N	File → New
Open the existing document	Ctrl+O	File → Open
Save a file	Ctrl+S	File → Save
Cut the selection	Ctrl+X	Edit → Cut
Copy the selection	Ctrl+C	Edit → Copy
Paste the cut or copied object	Ctrl+V	Edit → Paste
Reverses the last command performed	Ctrl+Z	Edit → Undo
Reverse the action performed by undo command	Ctrl+Y	Edit → Redo
Check spelling and grammar mistakes	F7	Tools → Spelling and grammar

Find and replace the text	Ctrl+H	Edit → Replace
Find a particular word	Ctrl+F	Edit → Find

NOTE: Use the same shortcut commands for file manipulation in MS Excel and in MS PowerPoint.

Overview of Spreadsheet

A spreadsheet is a collection of rows and columns forming a table. The intersection of each row and column is called a cell.

Commonly used terms in Spreadsheets

Worksheet (Spreadsheet): Worksheet refers to the row and column matrix sheet. They are used to list, organise and calculate the data.

Workbook: The files that are used in a spreadsheet are known as Workbooks, which are made up of worksheets or spreadsheets.

Cell: A cell is the basic unit of the spreadsheet. The intersection of a row and a column is called a cell.

Active cell or Selected cell: When you select a cell by clicking it with a mouse or move it with a keyboard, it becomes an active cell. It has a dark border around it.

Entering data into a Worksheet: Data can be entered into a worksheet by simply selecting a cell and then typing in it.

Overview of PowerPoint

A presentation is a systematic display of information using text, graphics, movies and sound. You can create a presentation by choosing one of these three options: Auto Content Wizard, Design Template, and Blank Presentation.

Adding text to a slide: Open the PowerPoint program. The new slide window will open. Select the title Slide layout which contains text boxes for a title and a subtitle. Type the text into these boxes.

Adding a new slide: Click on **Insert** menu and select **New Slide** option. The new slide dialog box appears.

OR

Press the shortcut keys **CTRL + M** to insert the new slide.

Chapter 1

MS WORD-II

WORKING WITH LISTS AND TABLES

- **Bulleted and numbered lists**
- **Nested lists**
- **Formatting lists**
- **Tables**

Learning Objective

To be able to work with tables and lists (bulleted as well as numbered) and to format them.

The bullets and numbering feature in Word help us to make our document more readable and easier to understand.

To create a bulleted or numbered list, use the Bullets and Numbering option from the Format menu.

Bulleted and Numbered Lists

1. Click the **Bulleted List** button (or) **Numbered List** button on the formatting toolbar.
2. Type the first entry and press **ENTER** Key. This will create a new bullet or a number on the next line.
3. Continue typing entries and press **ENTER** Key twice to end the list when you are finished with typing.

NOTE: If you want to start a new line without adding another bullet or number, hold down the **SHIFT** key while pressing **ENTER** Key.

Use the **Increase Indent** and **Decrease Indent** buttons on the formatting toolbar to create lists of multiple levels.

NOTE: You can type the text first, then highlight the section and click on the **Bulleted List** or **Numbered List** buttons to add bullets or numbers.

Example:

Bulleted List

Different realms of the earth

The three realms of the earth are:

- Lithosphere
- Atmosphere
- Hydrosphere

Numbered List

Different realms of the earth

The three realms of the earth are:

1. Lithosphere
2. Atmosphere
3. Hydrosphere

Nested Lists

To create a nested list, such as a numbered list under a bulleted list, follow these steps:

Type the list and increase the indentation of the items that will make up the nested list by clicking the **Increase Indent** button for each item.

Select the items and click on the Numbered List button present on the formatting toolbar.

Example:

● **ATMOSPHERE**	● **ATMOSPHERE**
• Troposphere	1. Troposphere
• Stratosphere	2. Stratosphere
• Ionosphere	3. Ionosphere
• Exosphere	4. Exosphere

The Numbered List has been applied.

Formatting Lists

The bullet and numbering format can be changed by using the **Bullets and Numbering** dialog box.

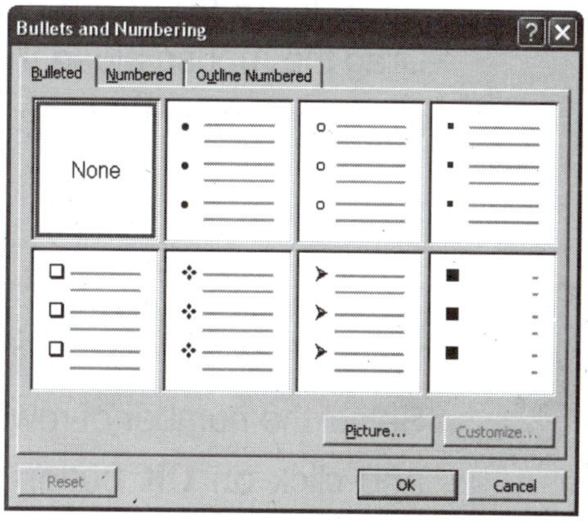

Bullets and Numbering

1. Select the entire list to change all the bullets or numbers.

   OR

   Place the cursor on a line in the list to change a single bullet.
2. Click on **Format → Bullets and Numbering** option from the menu bar.

   OR

   Right-click within the list and select **Bullets and Numbering** from the shortcut menu.
3. Select the list style from one of the seven choices given.

   OR

   Click the **Picture** button to choose a different icon. Click the **Numbered** tab to choose a numbered list style.
4. Click on **OK** when finished.

Example:

Different realms of the earth	Different realms of the earth
The three realms of the earth are:	The three realms of the earth are:
➢ Lithosphere	i. Lithosphere
➢ Atmosphere	ii. Atmosphere
➢ Hydrosphere	iii. Hydrosphere

Tables

A combination of rows and columns is called a table, which is used to display data in a row and columnar format. Tables make the data look simple and are used in the design of calendars, report cards and school timetables. There is a separate menu for inserting and working on tables.

Inserting a table

There are two ways to add a table to the document.

1. Click on **Insert Table** button on the standard toolbar. Drag the mouse along the grid to select the number of rows and columns for a table.

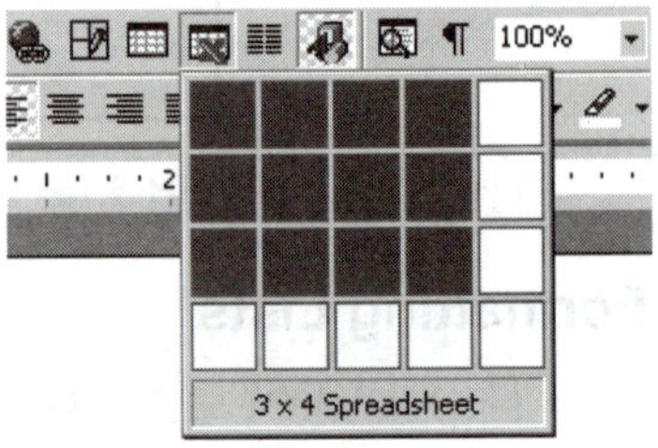

Insert table button

OR

2. Select **Table** → **Insert** → **Table** from the menu bar. The **Insert Table** dialog box appears.

   Select the number of rows and columns for the table and click on **OK** button.

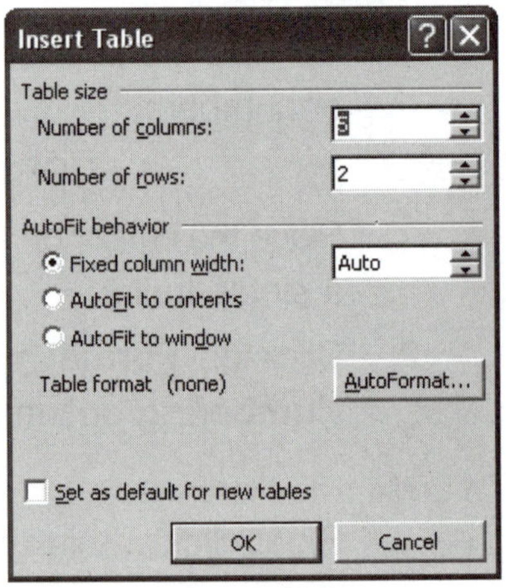

Insert table dialog box

To draw a table

Here, let us learn to draw a table.

- Select **Table** → **Draw Table** from the menu bar. The cursor turns into an image of a pencil and the **Tables and Borders** toolbar will appear on screen.
- Draw the cells of a table with the mouse. If you make a mistake, click the **Eraser**  button and drag the mouse over the area to be deleted.

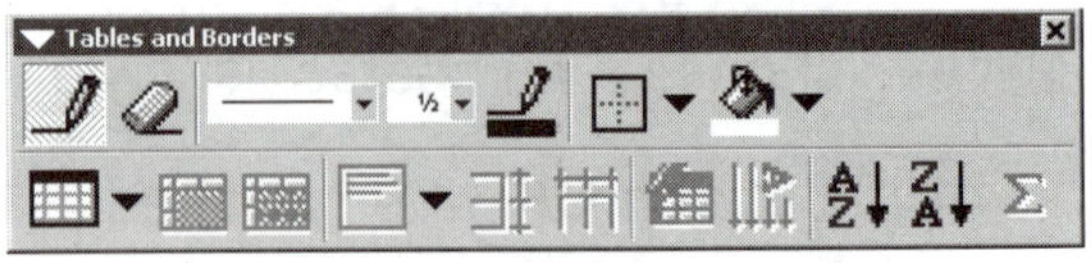

Tables and Border toolbar

- To draw more cells, click on the **Draw Table** button .

To come out from the drawing mode to normal typing mode press Esc (Escape) key.

Inserting rows and columns

Once the table is drawn, insert additional rows by placing the cursor in the row you want the additional rows above or below.

1. Select **Table → Insert → Rows Above or Rows Below**.

OR

2. Select an entire row and right-click with the mouse. Choose **Insert Rows** from the shortcut menu.

   Much like inserting a row, add a new column by placing the cursor in a cell adjacent to where the new column will be added.

1. Select **Table → Insert → Columns to the Left or Columns to the Right**.

OR

2. Select the column, right-click with the mouse and select **Insert Columns**.

Moving and Resizing a Table

A four-sided moving arrow and open box resizing handle will appear on the corners of the table as shown when the mouse is placed over the table. Click and drag the four-ended arrow to move the table and release the mouse button when the table is positioned in its place.

Click and drag the open box handle to resize the table. Change the column widths and row heights by clicking the cell dividers and dragging them with the mouse.

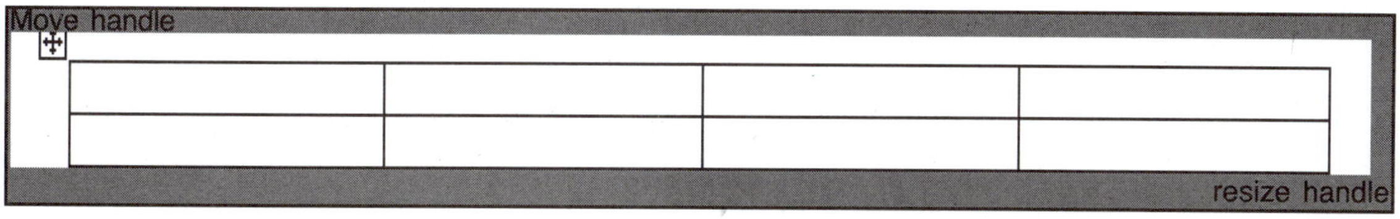

NOTE: To select the entire table, click the four-pointed arrow in a box over the top left hand corner of the table, which appears as your cursor nears the top of the table.

Tables and Borders Toolbar

The Tables and Borders toolbar helps to add border styles, shading, text effects, alignment and more options to a table. Access the toolbar by selecting

Table → Draw Table.

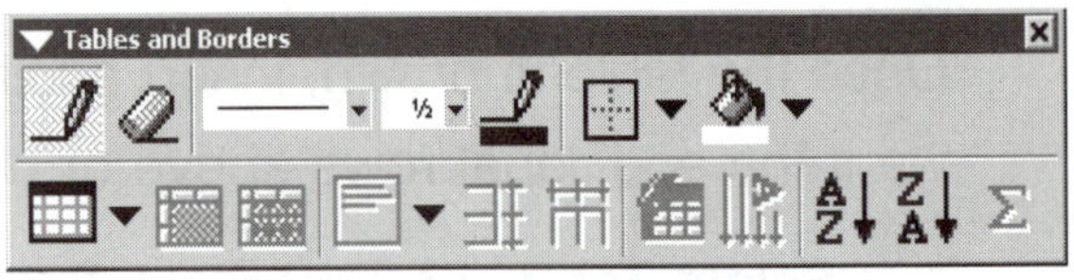

Tables and borders toolbar

OR

To activate the tables and borders toolbar select **View → Toolbars → Tables and Borders**.

Formatting a table

You need to select the cells of a table that you want to format. Click and drag the mouse over the cells or access the following command from the Table menu.

Selection	Menu Method	Mouse Method
One cell	Table → Select → Cell	Click the bottom, left corner of the cell when a black arrow appears.
One row	Table → Select → Row	Click outside the table to the left of the row.
One column	Table → Select →Column	Click outside the table above the column when a black arrow appears.
Several rows	(none)	Click outside the table to the left of the row and drag the mouse down.
Several columns	(none)	Click outside the table above the column.
Entire table	Table → Select → Table	Click on the four sided moving arrow of the table.

NOTE: You can use the **Tab** key to move to the next cell.

Table Properties

Use the **Table Properties** dialog box to set the table alignment, wrap text, apply borders and shading, set height and width of rows and columns, etc.

Access the box by selecting **Tables → Table Properties**.

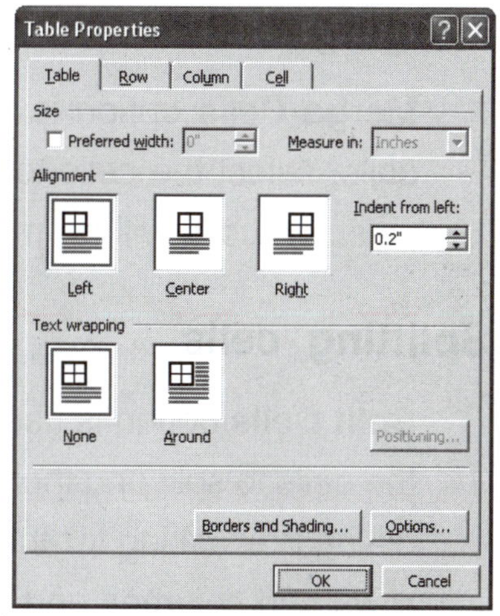

Table Properties

- **Size** - Check the **Preferred width** box and enter a value for the table to have an exact width.
- **Alignment** - Select the illustration that represents the alignment of the table in relation to the text of the document.
- **Text wrapping** - Select "None" if the table should appear on a separate line from the text or choose "Around" if the text should wrap around the table.
- **Borders and Shading** - Select from a number of border styles, colours and widths. Click the **shading** tab to change the background colour and pattern.

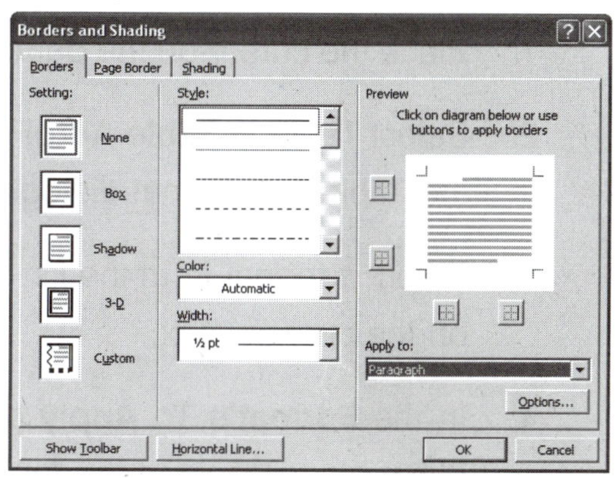

Borders

- **Options** - To change the spacing between the document text and the table borders under **Default cell margins**, click the Options button on the Table Properties window. Check the **Allow spacing between cells** box and enter a value to add space between the table cells.

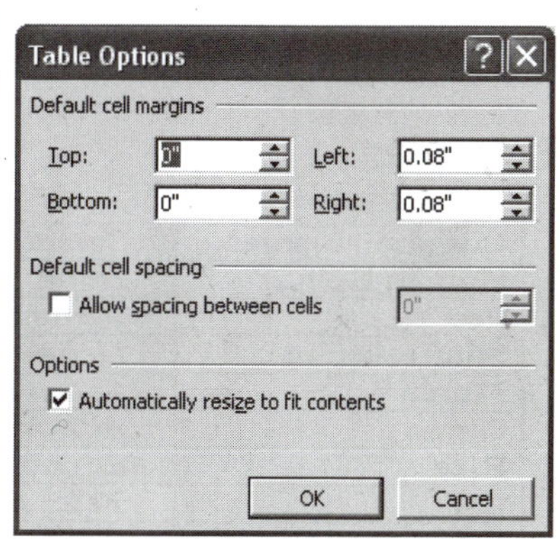

Table Options

Merging cells

Merge Cells option is used to combine two or more cells into one cell. To merge cells, select the cells to merge and then click on **Table → Merge cells** options. The selected cells will be merged.

Splitting cells

Split Cells option is used to split the cell(s) into two or more rows or columns. Select the cells to split and then click on **Table → Split cells** Option. It will display a Split cells dialog box asking for the number of rows and columns to split. Specify the number of rows and columns and click on OK button.

AutoFormat

The AutoFormat feature inserts the ready-made table format.

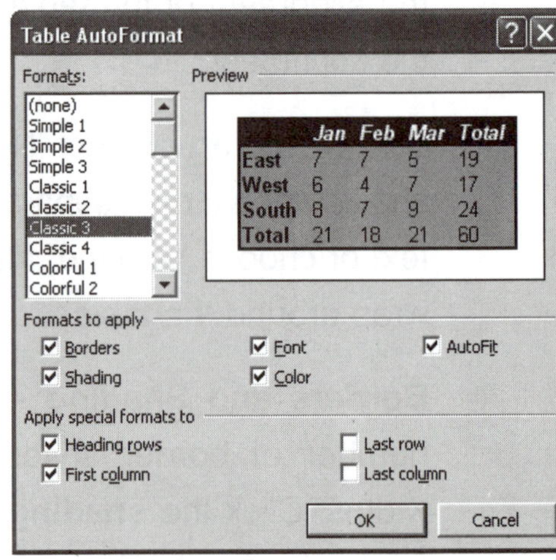

Table Autoformat

1. Place the cursor on the data inside the table.
2. Select **Table → Table AutoFormat** to display the Table Autoformat dialog box appears.
3. Select a format from the list that is displayed on the preview box.
4. In the **Format's To Apply** group, select the elements to apply to the table.
5. In the **Apply special formats to**, select the parts of the table to be formatted.
6. Click on **OK** button.

Example:

Common Names	Scientific names
Human Beings	*Homo sapiens*
Pea	*Pisum sativum*
Sunflower	*Helianthus annuus*
Potato	*Solanum tuberosum*
Onion	*Allium cepa*
Rice	*Oryza sativa*
Cat	*Felis domesticus*
Dog	*Canis familaris*

Common Names	*Scientific names*
Human Beings	*Homo sapiens*
Pea	*Pisum sativum*
Sunflower	*Helianthus annuus*
Potato	*Solanum tuberosum*
Onion	*Allium cepa*
Rice	*Oryza sativa*
Cat	*Felis domesticus*
Dog	*Canis familiaris*

Converting existing text to a table

You can convert the existing text to a table format without drawing a table and entering the data again.

1. Select the text to convert it to a table.
2. Select **Table** → **Convert** → **Text to Table** option.
3. Choose the number of columns and number of rows to be divided.
4. Select the text to be arranged in the columns and rows.
5. Choose **OK**.

Example:

Organism **Life span**
Lion 20–25 yrs
Horse 25–30 yrs
Ostrich 50 yrs
Human Beings 60–70 yrs
Elephant 70–90 yrs
Tortoise 120–150 yrs

Organism	Life span
Lion	20–25 yrs
Horse	25–30 yrs
Ostrich	50 yrs
Human Beings	60–70 yrs
Elephant	70–90 yrs
Tortoise	120–150 yrs

Converting a table to ordinary text

You can convert an existing table to ordinary text without having to re-type the data.

1. Select the entire table.
2. Select **Table** → **Convert** → **Table to Text** option to display a **Table to Text** dialog box.
3. Select the text to be separated (paragraph marks are best for continuous text).
4. Choose **OK**.

Example:

Organism	Life span
Lion	20–25 yrs
Horse	25–30 yrs
Ostrich	50 yrs
Human Beings	60–70 yrs
Elephant	70–90 yrs
Tortoise	120–150 yrs

Organism **Life span**
Lion 20–25 yrs
Horse 25–30 yrs
Ostrich 50 yrs
Human Beings 60–70 yrs
Elephant 70–90 yrs
Tortoise 120–150 yrs

Formulae in a table

Word can also do simple calculations on a table like finding the sum of column, calculating product of two cells, finding the maximum or minimum in a column or row. Word uses code to refer to the cells, i.e. rows and columns. **Letters** are used to refer to **columns**, and **numbers** are used to refer to **rows** and for a cell the combination of respective column letter and row number is used. For Example, first column in table is A, second column is B and so on. First row in table is 1, second is 2 and so on. Thus, the reference to the first cell is A1 and the reference to the first cell in second column is B1 and so on.

	A	B	C	D
1	A1	B1	C1	D1
2	A2			
3	A3			
4				

NOTE: A formula will begin with an **Equal (=)** sign.

To apply formulae

1. Position the cursor in the cell where the answer should appear.
2. Select **Table → Formula** to open the formula dialog box.
3. Select the required formula from the **Paste function** box. By default sum function will be displayed on the formula bar.

   E.g., = SUM(), = Average()
4. Select a number format.
5. Choose **OK**.

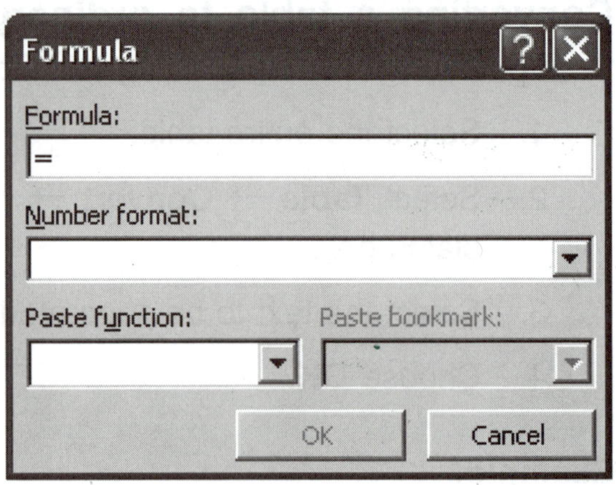

Formula dialog box

Summary

The data can be presented in rows and columns by creating a table.

- Intersection of a row and a column is called a cell.
- The table can be formatted.
- You can insert or delete rows and columns.
- Existing text can be converted into table and vice-versa.
- You can apply simple formulae in a table.

Exercises

1. Fill in the blanks.

a. Bulleted list button is present on the ___formatting___ toolbar.

b. A combination of rows and columns is called a ___table___.

c. The table option is present in the ___insert___ menu.

d. The ___auto format___ feature is used to insert the ready-made table format.

2. Match the following.

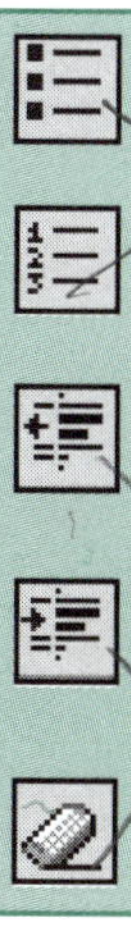

a.	i. Numbered list
b.	ii. Bulleted list
c.	iii. Eraser button
d.	iv. Decrease indent
e.	v. Increase indent

3. State whether true [✔] or false [✕].

a. The insert table button is present on the formatting toolbar.

b. The table can be moved and resized.

c. The rows and column can be inserted in a table.

d. Ordinary text cannot be converted into a table.

e. The AutoFormat option is present in the Table menu.

4. Crossword

Clues:

Across

1. Various patterns of bullets
2. Various patterns of numbers

Down

3. The vertical lines of cells
4. The horizontal lines of cells
5. A combination of row and columns

5. Answer the following questions.

a. What are the steps to create Bulleted and Numbered lists?

b. What are the steps to insert a table?

c. What are the steps to insert rows and columns?

d. What are the steps to apply styles to a table using table AutoFormat?

Lab Activity

I. Type the paragraph and perform the following operations.

The Solar System

Our solar system consists of the sun, nine planets and their natural satellites, countless asteroids and comets, all of them are revolving around the sun in their respective paths called orbits. The word 'planet' comes from a Greek word meaning 'wanderer'. There are nine planets in our solar system. Unlike the sun and other stars, planets do not have light of their own. Planets shine because they reflect the sun's light. In the order of their distances from the sun, the nine planets are:

Mercury	Venus	Earth
Mars	Jupiter	Saturn
Uranus	Neptune	Pluto

1. Apply bullets or numbers to the nine planets and observe the difference.
2. Try applying different bullets and numbering styles.

II. Create the following table and save it in a new document.

Sl. No	Organism	Scientific name
1	Man	*Homo sapiens*
2	Cat	*Felis domestica*
3	Lion	*Felis leo*
4	Tiger	*Felis tigris*
5	Mango	*Mangifera indica*
6	Banyan	*Ficus bengalensis*
7	Pea	*Pisum sativum*
8	Radish	*Raphanus sativum*

1. Add borders to the above table.
2. Align the table to the center.
3. Resize the columns to fit the text.
4. Centre align the first column and make the column headings bold.
5. Insert a row after fourth row and enter one more organism's information.

III. Create the following table and perform the following operations.

Sl. No	Units	Symbol
1	Meter	m
2	Decimeter	dm
3	Centimeter	cm
4	Millimeter	mm
5	Kilometer	km

1. Add borders to the table.
2. Resize the table.
3. Insert a column after the second column.
4. Select a format for the table using AutoFormat feature.

Chapter 2

MS WORD-II

WORKING WITH GRAPHICS

- Bitmap and Vector graphics
- Adding ClipArt and Images
- Editing graphics
- AutoShapes
- WordArt
- Special characters

Learning Objective

To learn to insert and edit different types of graphics and to work with AutoShapes.

Word supports different types of picture formats. Adding graphics to the document makes it more effective. Word has a built-in drawing toolbar which allows you to draw objects.

There are two types of graphics formats:

1. Bitmap graphics
2. Vector graphics

Bitmap graphics

Bitmap graphics are also called pixels. They are composed of small dots, which define colour and intensity. Paint brush is an example of bitmap graphics.

Vector graphics

Vector graphics are composed of a set of drawing instructions of an object like circle or rectangle and are represented in co-ordinates form. The resolution of a vector image is not fixed. Vector graphics can be enlarged or reduced.

Word line art or graphics created using word graphics toolbar are examples of vector graphics, which take less disk space compared to bitmap graphics because the objects are stored as command rather than images.

Adding ClipArt and Images

ClipArt

The ClipArt feature allows you to add images to the document. ClipArt often helps to convey messages more effeciently. The ClipArt gallery includes sound and motion clips which can be inserted in the document.

Adding ClipArt

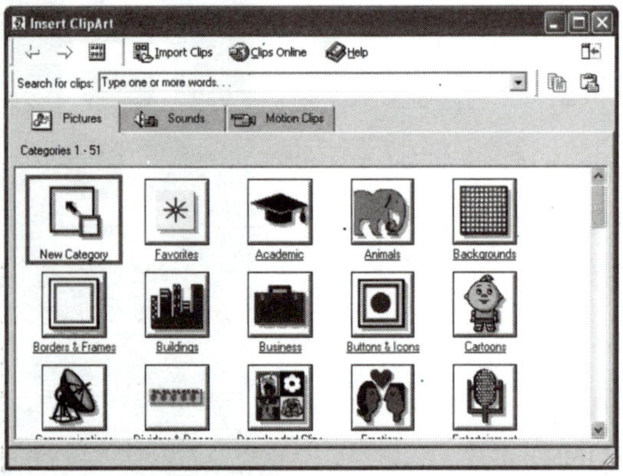

Insert ClipArt dialog box

To add a ClipArt image from the Microsoft library to a document, follow these steps:

- Select **Insert → Picture → ClipArt** from the menu bar.
- To find an image, click in the **Search for clip** combo box**.** Delete the words "Type one or more words ..." and enter keywords describing the image you want to use.

OR

Click one of the category icons.

- Click on the image you want to add in the document and the following menu will appear.

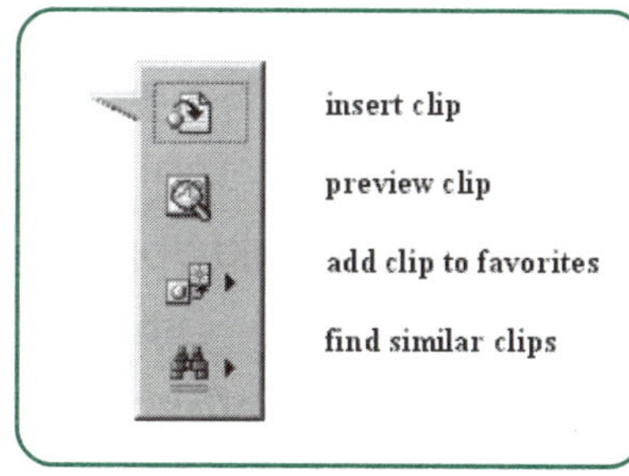

- Click on **Insert Clip** to add the image in the document.
- **Preview Clip** to view the image full-size before adding it to the document.
- Drag the bottom, right corner of the preview window to resize the image and click the ☒ close button to end the preview.
- **Add Clip to Favorites** will add the selected image to your favourites directory that can be chosen from the **Insert ClipArt** dialog box.

- **Find Similar Clips** will retrieve images similar to the one you have chosen.
- Continue selecting images to add in the document and click the **Close** button in the top, right corner of the **Insert ClipArt** window to stop adding ClipArt in the document.

Add an image from a file

To add image from a flie, follow these steps:

- Select **Insert** → **Picture** → **From File** on the menu bar.
- Click the down arrow button on the right of the **Look in** window to find the image on your computer.
- Select the file name from the list and click the **insert** button.

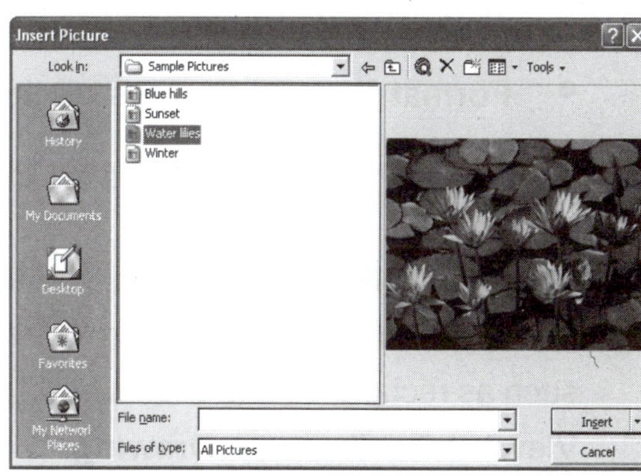

Insert Picture dialog box

Editing Graphics

Activate the image you want to edit by clicking on it once using the mouse. Nine handles will appear around the graphic. Click and drag these handles to resize the image. The handles on the corners will resize proportionally while the handles on the straight lines stretch the image. More picture effects can be applied using the Picture toolbar. The **Picture toolbar** should appear when you click on the image. Otherwise, select **View → Toolbars → Picture** from the menu bar to activate it.

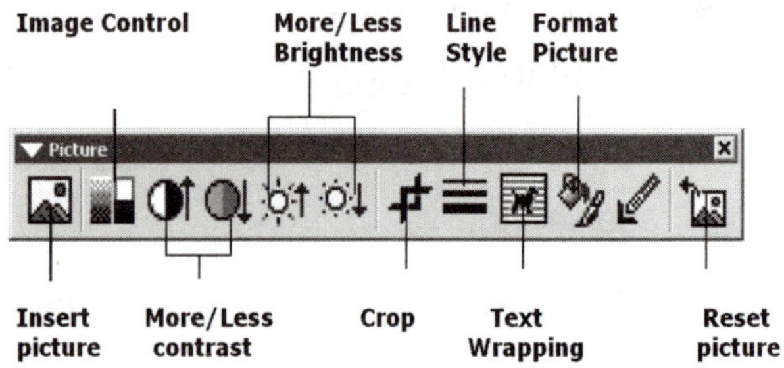

Picture toolbar

- **Insert Picture** will display the image selection window and allow you to change the image.
- **Image Control** allows you to make the image grayscale, black and white or a watermark.
- **More/Less Contrast** modifies the contrast between the colours of the image.
- **More/Less Brightness** darkens or brightens the image.
- Click **Crop** and drag the handles on the activated image to delete outer portions of the image.
- **Line Style** will add a variety of borders to the graphics.
- **Text Wrapping** makes the document to wrap around the graphics.
- **Format Picture** displays all the image properties in a separate window.
- **Reset Picture** will delete all the modifications made to the image.

Drawing Toolbar

MS Word's drawing toolbar provides tools for creating lines, arrows and basic shapes such as rectangles and circles etc. To display the drawing toolbar, select **View → Toolbars → Drawing**.

Drawing toolbar

AutoShapes

The AutoShapes toolbar allows you to draw many different geometrical shapes, arrows, flow chart symbols, stars and banners on the document. It is very useful in designing and giving an impact to your document. Activate the AutoShapes toolbar by selecting **Insert → Picture → AutoShapes** or **View → Toolbars → AutoShapes** from the menubar or clicking the **AutoShapes** button on the drawing toolbar. Click each button on the toolbar to view the options for drawing the shape.

- **Lines -** After clicking the Lines button on the AutoShapes toolbar, draw a **straight line, arrow or double-ended arrow** from the first row of options by clicking the respective button. Click in the document where you would like the line to begin and click again where you would like it to end. To draw a curved line or **freeform shape,** select curved lines from the menu (first and second buttons of second row), click in the document where you want the line to appear and click the mouse every time you want a curve to begin. End creating the graphic by clicking on the starting end or pressing the **ESC** key.

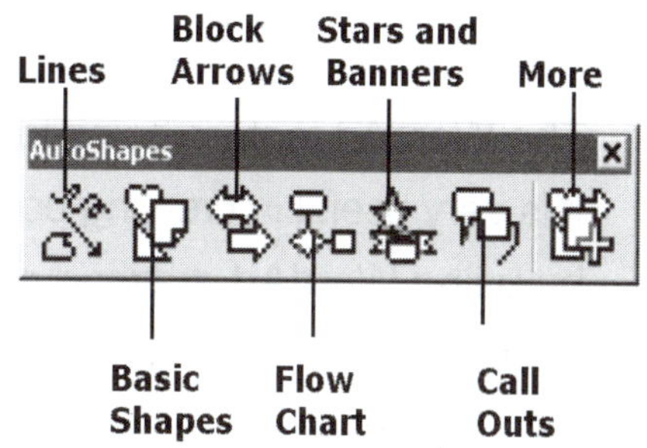

AutoShapes toolbar

- **Basic Shapes -** Click the Basic Shapes button on the AutoShapes toolbar to select from many **two and three-dimensional shapes, icons, braces and brackets.** Use the drag-and-drop method to draw the shape in the document. When the shape has been drawn, it can be resized using the open box handles and other adjustments specific to each shape can be made using the yellow diamond handles.

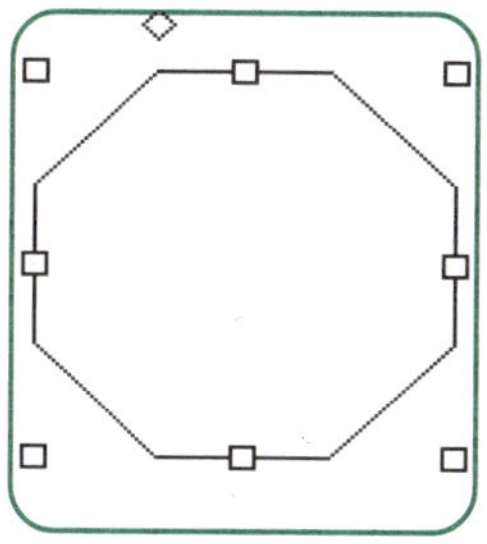

- **Block Arrows -** Select Block Arrows to choose from many types of **two and three-dimensional arrows.** Drag-and-drop the arrow in the document and use the open box and yellow diamond handles to adjust the arrowheads.

  Each AutoShape can also be rotated by first clicking the **Free Rotate** button on the drawing toolbar. Click and drag the green handles around the image to rotate it.

- **Flowchart** - It allows you to add flow chart symbols to the document and use the line to draw connections between the symbols.

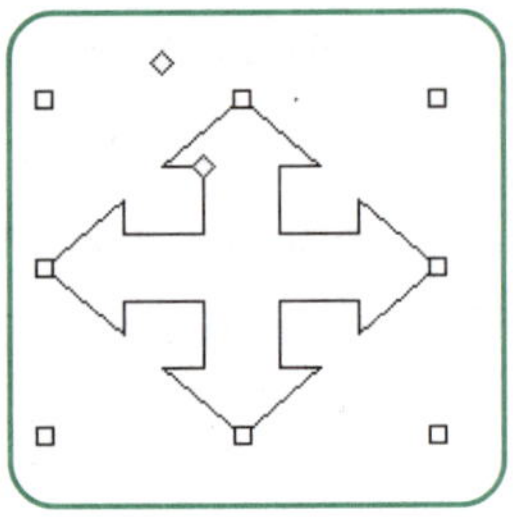

- **Stars and Banners** - Click the button to select stars, bursts, banners and scrolls.
- **Call Outs** - Select from the speech and thought bubbles and line call outs. Enter the call out text in the text box.
- **More AutoShapes** - Click this button to choose from a list of ClipArt categories.

WordArt

The WordArt feature helps to create artistic text that makes the document look attractive. It is very useful in creating posters and greeting cards. You can use this in your document by using WordArt drawing styles or by using the WordArt button with added features, such as 3D effects and textured fills.

Inserting WordArt drawing object

- Click on **Insert → Picture → WordArt** from menu bar, a WordArt gallery is displayed as shown.
- Select the type of WordArt drawing style you want to use and then click OK.
- In the Edit WordArt Text dialog box, type the text you want to format and click OK.

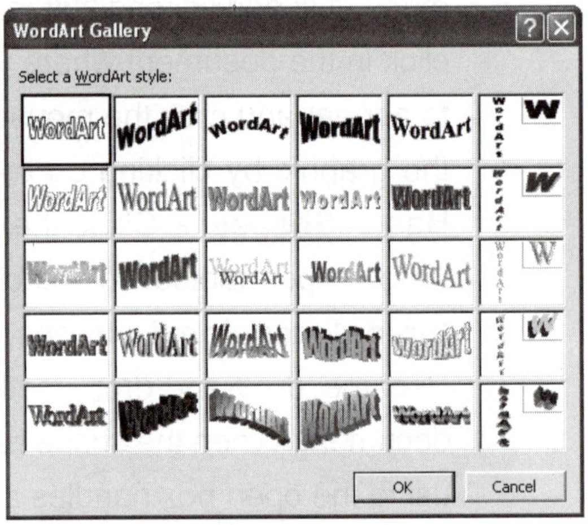

WordArt Gallery

Example:

WordArt Text

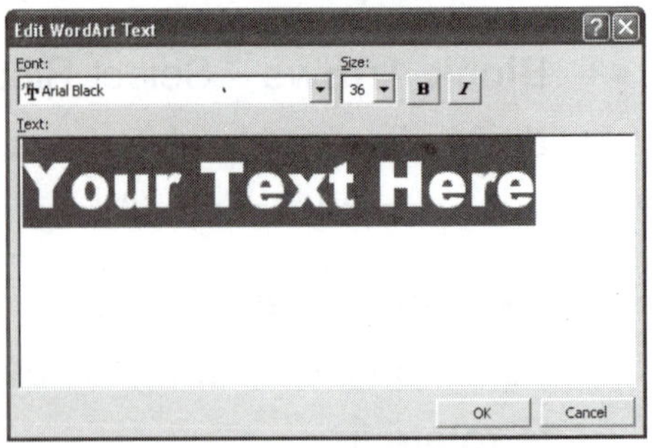

Edit WordArt Text window

NOTE: You can also click the WordArt button on the drawing toolbar at the bottom of the MS Word screen to get the WordArt gallery.

Inserting Symbols and Special Charcters

Special symbols such as trade mark symbols special characters, bullets and the frequently used symbols can be inserted using **Symbol** command.

1. Select **Insert** → **Symbol**. A symbol dialog box is displayed.
2. Click on the symbol to see enlarged view.

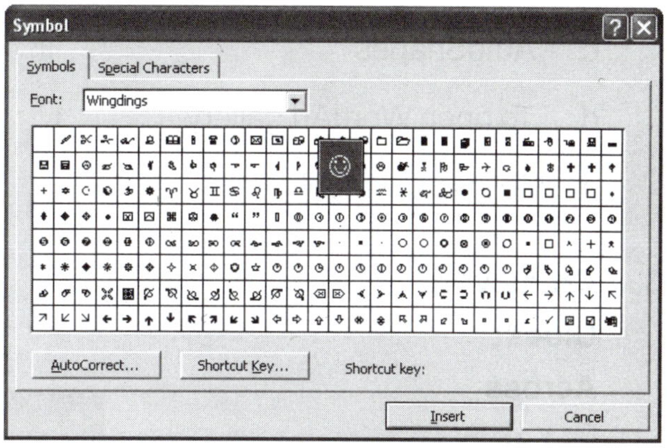

Symbol dialog box

3. Click on **Insert** button to place the selected symbols on the document.

Summary

- Word offers graphics in documents to enhance the appearence of the document.
- ClipArt allows us to add images to the document.
- Pictures can also be inserted from the other picture files.
- The AutoShapes toolbar can be used to draw many different geometrical shapes, arrows, flowchart symbols, stars and banners on the document.
- The WordArt feature helps to create special effects to the text and to make it look attractive.

Exercises

1. Fill in the blanks.

a. ClipArt option is present in the ____________ menu.

b. The ____________ toolbar allow us to draw the different geometrical shapes, arrows, flowchart symbols, stars and banners on the document.

c. The ____________ feature helps to create artistic text.

2. Match the following.

a.	To add a ClipArt	i.	Insert → Picture → From file
b.	To add an image from a file	ii.	Insert → Picture → AutoShapes
c.	AutoShapes	iii.	Insert → Picture → ClipArt
d.	To open WordArt gallery	iv.	Insert → Symbol
e.	To insert symbols	v.	Insert → Picture → WordArt

3. Crossword

Clues:

Across

1. Shapes can be inserted automatically without drawing
2. Making changes to the existing document

Down

3. Used to create artistic text
4. Option which allows us to add images to the document
5. The fourth menu on the menubar

4. State whether true [✔] or false [✕].

a. ClipArt feature helps us to add images to the document.

b. View menu is used to add pictures from a file.

c. Symbols and special characters can be inserted.

d. Pictures can be inserted from the other applications.

e. The WordArt feature helps to create special effects to the text and make it look attractive.

5. Answer the following questions.

a. What are the steps to add ClipArt?

b. What are the steps to add an image from a file?

c. What are the steps to insert WordArt?

Lab Activity

I. Create a document on the topic "Our Universe" and insert related ClipArt. Use WordArt, Symbols and AutoShapes to give an impressive look to the document.

II. Create a document on the topic "Water" and insert ClipArt. Make use of WordArt to give an artistic look to your document.

III. Insert the following ClipArts in your document.

IV. Insert the following symbols in your document.

■ ✈ ✵ ● □ ❖

V. Insert the following AutoShapes into your document.

VI. Insert the following text using WordArt.

Digestive system, Respiratory system, Circulatory system, Nervous system

VII. Design a greeting card for your friend's birthday.

VIII. Insert an image in a document and edit it.

FINGER STRETCH

Extend, separate fingers and stretch; hold for five seconds; relax and gently bend fingers.

Chapter 3

MS EXCEL-II

WORKING WITH BASIC FORMULAE

- **Cell References**
- **Basic Formulae**
- **Functions**

Learning Objective

To learn to use basic formulae in Excel.

The most powerful feature of Excel is its ability to do fast and accurate calculations. To make calculative work, we require a formula which refers to the cell address.

Cell References

A reference identifies a cell or a range of cells on a worksheet and tells Microsoft Excel where to look for the values or data you want to use in a formula. With references, you can use data contained in different parts of a worksheet in one formula or use the value from one cell in several formulae.

By default, Excel uses the **A1 reference style**, which refers to columns with letters (A through IV, for a total of 256 columns) and refers to rows with numbers (1 through 65,536). These letters and numbers are called row and column headings. To refer a cell, enter the column letter followed by the row number.

For example:

D50 refers to the cell at the intersection of column D and row 50.

To refer to a range of cells, enter the reference for the cell in the upper-left corner of the range, a colon (:) and then the reference to the cell in the lower-right corner of the range. The following are examples of references.

To refer to	Use
The cell in column A and row 10	A10
The range of cells in column A and rows 10 through 20	A10:A20
The range of cells in row 15 and columns B through E	B15:E15
All cells in row 5	5:5
All cells in columns H through J	H:J
All cells in columns A to E and rows 10 to 20	A10:E20

There are three types of cell references:

1. Relative references E.g: G9
2. Absolute references E.g: G9
3. Mixed references E.g: $G9 Or G$9

1. Relative Cell Referencing

D2 =B2+C2

	A	B	C	D
1	Name	Basic	Allowance	GrossSal
2	A	1000	200	1200
3	B	1200	250	
4	C	1300	150	

Here, cells B2 and C2 are known as relative addresses.

	A	B	C	D
1	Name	Basic	Allowance	GrossSal
2	A	1000	200	1200
3	B	1200	250	1450
4	C	1300	150	1450

The formula will be copied from D2 to D4.

2. Absolute Cell Referencing

Consider the example given below:

	A	B	C	D
1			Grace:	5
2	Name	Sub1	Sub 2	Total
3	..	.. ..	=B3+C3+D1	
4	..	.. ..		

In the above example, the total mark has to be added up with the grace mark 5 stored in cell D1 for each student. The D1 indicates the cell address is constant while copying the formula for the remaining records.

3. Mixed Cell Referencing

B2 =$A3*B$2

	A	B	C	D
1	10	11	12	
2	10	=$A3*B$2		
3	11			
4	12			

$A fixes the reference absolutely on column A, which contains one set of values to be multiplied. $2 fixes the reference absolutely on row 2, which contains the other set of values to be multiplied. Drag the handle on cell B2 so that the border expands, extending the selection to cell D4 and copying the formula across. Drag the handle on the selections B3:D3 down so that it extends the selection down to row 5 and copies the formulae to the adjacent rows.

Basic Formulae

A formulae can consist of operators (+ addition, – subtraction, * multiplication, / division), cell address or values. It starts with an **equal to (=)** sign. For example, if you want to add two numbers say 40 and 60:

Enter 40 in cell A; Enter 60 in cell A2.

Now in A3 enter the formula as '= 40 + 60' and press the enter key.

Immediately the result 100 will be displayed in the cell A3.

In the above example, we have used numbers. But it is preferable to use a cell reference in formulae.

For example:

To calculate the total marks scored by a student whose marks are as shown below.

G2 =

	A	B	C	D	E	F	G
1	**Name**	**English**	**Maths**	**Science**	**Social**	**Computer**	**Total**
2	John	45	65	30	56	77	

We first enter the formula = B2+C2+D2+E2+F2, in G2 cell and press the enter key. These are the cell addresses of the corresponding numbers.

	A	B	C	D	E	F	G
1	**Name**	**English**	**Maths**	**Science**	**Social**	**Computer**	**Total**
2	John	45	65	30	56	77	=B2+C2+D2+E2+F2

The **Total** is displayed in the same cell G2. The advantage of using a formula is that it can be applied to many more calculations, for example, the total marks of all the students.

To find the total marks of all the students, click on the result cell H2. A plus sign appears (+).

SUM | =B2+C2+D2+E2+F2

	A	B	C	D	E	F	G
1	Name	English	Maths	Science	Social	Computer	Total
2	John	45	65	30	56	77	=B2+C2+D2+E2+F2
3	Benny	80	35	45	90	55	
4	Jim	55	50	75	85	95	
5	Mary	88	77	66	55	85	

Drag it to the next cell up to the last record, G8. Automatically the total will be calculated and displayed.

G2 | =B2+C2+D2+E2+F2

	A	B	C	D	E	F	G
1	Name	English	Maths	Science	Social	Computer	Total
2	John	45	65	30	56	77	273
3	Benny	80	35	45	90	55	305
4	Jim	55	50	75	85	95	360
5	Mary	88	77	66	55	85	371

How to copy and paste the formula:

1. Select the cell which contains the formula.
2. Click on the **Edit** → **Copy** option.
3. Click on the cell where you want the formula to be pasted.
4. Click on the **Edit** → **Paste** option.

The formula is copied. Repeat the above steps to apply the same formula to the other cells.

Functions

A Function is a pre-defined formula for performing a particular task. Excel provides many such functions to make work easier.

SUM

The general form of Sum function is:

'=SUM(Starting cell : Ending cell)'

This function adds all the numbers stored in the selected cells.

1. Type '=' sign in the cell to get answer.
2. Type SUM and open the left bracket =SUM(.
3. Select the range of cells for which you want to calculate the sum.
4. Close the right bracket).
5. Press Enter key to get the result.

	A	B	C	D	E	F	G
1	Name	English	Maths	Science	Social	Computer	Total
2	John	45	65	30	56	77	=SUM(B2:F2)
3	Benny	80	35	45	90	55	

Sum Function

AUTOSUM

The AutoSum button on toolbar automatically calculates the sum of numbers. Click on AutoSum button on standard toolbar to calculate the total of the set of numbers. This button gives the sum of values of selected cells without typing the formula.

AuoSum Function

AutoSum

AVERAGE

This function gives you the average of series of numbers. The general form of this function is:

'=AVERAGE(Starting cell : Ending cell)'

	A	B	C	D	E	F	G	H
1	Name	English	Maths	Science	Social	Computer	Total	Average
2	John	45	65	30	56	77	273	=AVERAGE(B2:F2)

Type the formula as shown and press enter key. You will get the average of series of numbers in the cell H2.

	A	B	C	D	E	F	G	H
1	**Name**	**English**	**Maths**	**Science**	**Social**	**Computer**	**Total**	**Average**
2	John	45	65	30	56	77	273	54.6

Average Function

MAXIMUM

This function is used for finding the largest value from a given series of numbers. The general form of this function is:

'=MAX(Starting cell : Ending cell)'

	A	B	C	D	E	F	G	H
1	**Name**	**English**	**Maths**	**Science**	**Social**	**Computer**	**Total**	**Maximum**
2	John	45	65	30	56	77	273	=MAX(B2:F2)

If you type the formula as shown, the result will be:

	A	B	C	D	E	F	G	H
1	**Name**	**English**	**Maths**	**Science**	**Social**	**Computer**	**Total**	**Maximum**
2	John	45	65	30	56	77	273	77

Maximum Function

MINIMUM

This function gives the smallest value from a set of values. The general form of this functions:

'=MIN(Starting cell : Ending cell)'

	A	B	C	D	E	F	G	H
1	**Name**	**English**	**Maths**	**Science**	**Social**	**Computer**	**Total**	**Minimum**
2	John	45	65	30	56	77	273	=MIN(B2:F2)

If you type the formula shown, the result will be:

	A	B	C	D	E	F	G	H
1	**Name**	**English**	**Maths**	**Science**	**Social**	**Computer**	**Total**	**Minimum**
2	John	45	65	30	56	77	273	30

Minimum Function

COUNT

This function counts the number of selected cells that contain data. The general form of this function is:

'=COUNT(Starting cell : Ending cell)'

SUM ▾ X ✓ = =COUNT(F2:F5)

	A	B	C	D	E	F	G
1	**Name**	**English**	**Maths**	**Science**	**Social**	**Computer**	**Total**
2	John	45	65	30	56	77	273
3	Benny	80	35	45	90	55	305
4	Jim	55	50	75	85	95	360
5	Mary	88	77	66	55	85	371
6							
7						=COUNT(F2:F5)	

Type the formula as shown and the result will be '4' because the number of cells that contain data between F2 and F5 are 4.

F7 ▾ = =COUNT(F2:F5)

	A	B	C	D	E	F	G
1	**Name**	**English**	**Maths**	**Science**	**Social**	**Computer**	**Total**
2	John	45	65	30	56	77	273
3	Benny	80	35	45	90	55	305
4	Jim	55	50	75	85	95	360
5	Mary	88	77	66	55	85	371
6							
7						4	

Count Function

Summary

- The most powerful feature of Excel is its ability to do fast and accurate calculations.
- A formula consists of operators (+ addition, – subtraction, * multiplication, / division), cell address or values.
- A function is a pre-defined formula for performing a particular task.
- The AutoSum button automatically calculates the sum of the numbers.

Exercises

1. Answer the following questions.

a. What are cell references?

b. What is a formula?

c. What are functions?

d. Explain the AutoSum feature of Excel.

e. Explain some of the basic functions that are present in Excel.

2. Match the following.

	A		B
a.	COUNT(A2:A6)	i.	Unknown formula
b.	SUM(D2:G2)	ii.	Finds the least number in the range
c.	AVERAGE(D2:G2)	iii.	Counts the number of selected cells that contain data
d.	MAXIMUM(A2:A6)	iv.	Finds the addition of numbers
e.	MIN(A2:A6)	v.	Finds the average of numbers

3. Write the formulae and functions of the following terms.

a. Sum　　b. Average　　c. Maximum　　d. Minimum

4. Crossword

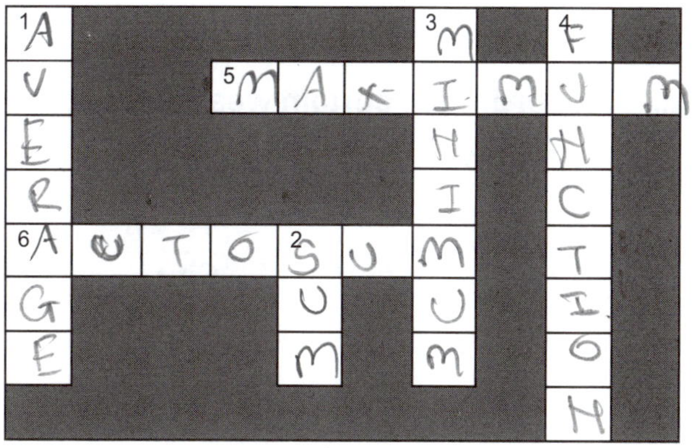

Clues:

Across

5. The function used for finding the largest value from a given set of numbers

6. It automaticlly calculates the sum of numbers

Down

1. This function gives the average of series of numbers
2. This function is used to add all the numbers
3. This function gives the smallest value from a set of numbers
4. The pre-defined formula for perfoming a particualr task

5. Fill in the blanks.

a. A ___function___ is a pre-defined formula for performing a particular task.

b. The ___autosum___ option automatically calculates the sum of numbers.

c. The ___count___ function counts the number of selected cells that contains data.

Lab Activity

I. Open a new workbook and enter the following data.

	A	B	C	D	E	F	G	H
1	**Name**	**English**	**Maths**	**Science**	**Social**	**Computer**	**Total**	**Average**
2	Richard	77	51	33	78	77		
3	John	80	35	45	90	55		
4	Ronald	66	85	65	95	66		
5	Ben	55	66	87	94	65		

For the above table, perform the following operations:

1. Find the total of all the subjects for Richard and John using formulae in total column.
2. Find the total of remaining students using AutoSum function.
3. Find the average of all the subjects in the average column.
4. Count the number of students present.

II. According to certain weather report the temperature of five metropolitan cities is as follows:

	A	B	C
1	**City**	**Maximum**	**Minimum**
2	California	30	26
3	Chicago	25	30
4	Los Angels	20	30
5	Delhi	20	25

1. Find the maximum temperature.
2. Find the minimum temperature.
3. Find the average temperature.

III. Open a new workbook, enter the following data and apply the formula for the given queries.

1. Find the Total sales of all products.

   (Hint: Total = Goods Sold * Selling Price)

2. Calculate the Amount Received as 60% of Total sales.
   (Hint: Amount Received = Total * 60/100)

	A	B	C	D	E	F	G	H
1	Sales Report							
2	Product Name	Total Goods	Sold Goods	Cost Price	Total	Amount Received	Balance Amount	Remaining Goods
3	Monitor	20	12	5000				
4	Keyboard	20	9	600				
5	Mouse	20	10	200				
6	CPU	20	12	10000				
7	Scanner	20	10	4000				
8	Printer	20	11	2500				
9	Joystick	20	15	250				
10	Speaker	20	15	400				

3. Calculate the Balance Amount to be paid.

   (Hint: Balance Amount = Total – Amount Received)

4. Find the remaining number of goods to be sold.

5. Save this workbook as 'sales.xls'.

IV. Find the missing number in the following table, using the given values of Length, Breadth and Area.

Formulae

Area = Length * Breadth

Length = Area / Breadth

Breadth = Area / Length

	A	B	C	D
1	Serial No	Lengths (in mts)	Breadth (in mts)	Area (in Sq.mts)
2	1	13	?	52
3	2	6	?	90
4	3	?	12	108
5	4	?	16	144
6	5	30	5	?
7	6	15	?	225
8	7	10	8	?
9	8	?	17	1700

V. Find the distance covered by each of the vehicles given in the following table.

(Hint: Speed = Distance/Time)

	A	B	C	D
1	**Vehicle**	**Time (in Hrs)**	**Speed (in Km/hr)**	**Distance (in Km)**
2	Cycle	10	60	
3	Scooter	5	80	
4	Car	8	100	
5	Van	12	110	
6	Bus	1	60	
7	Truck	3	70	
8	Train	10	120	
9	Aeroplane	5	150	

TORSO STRETCH

Raise elbows, without moving hips; turn upper body left. Hold still for a few seconds and then turn right. Hold still for a few seconds and repeat this three times.

Chapter 4

MS EXCEL-II

CONDITIONAL FORMATTING IN EXCEL

- AutoFormat
- Conditional Formatting

Learning Objectives

To learn how to apply AutoFormat and use Conditional Formatting in Excel.

Formatting the Spreadsheet

AutoFormat

An AutoFormat is a built-in table format, which can be applied to a range of cells. It automatically formats the data in a desired presentable form.

To apply the AutoFormat, follow the steps given below:

1. Select the range of cells you want to format.
2. Click on **Format** menu and select **AutoFormat**.
3. Select the format of your choice **Example** 'Colorful 3'.
4. Click on **OK** button to apply the format.

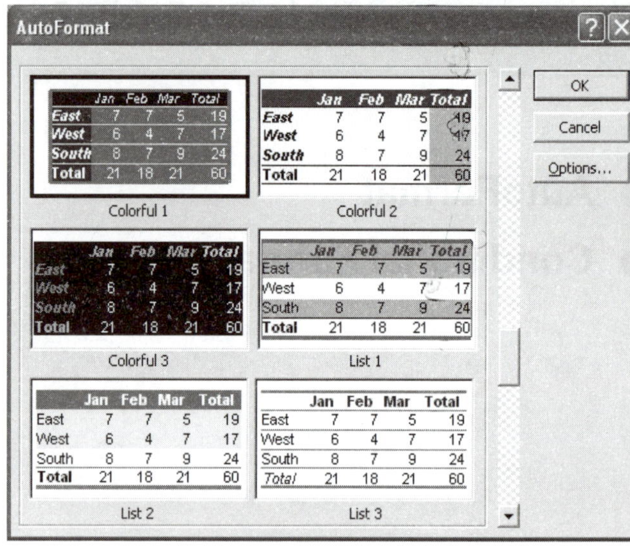

AutoFormat menu

Example:

60 minutes	1 minute
60 minutes	1 hour
24 hours	1 day
7 days	1 week
30 days	1 month
12 months	1 year
10 years	1 decade
100 years	1 centinary
1000 years	1 millennium

Table after applying AutoFormat option

Conditional Formatting

Conditional Formatting is a feature that allows you to format the data in a cell that satisfies certain condition.

	A	B	C	D	E	F
1	**Name**	**English**	**Maths**	**Science**	**Computers**	**Total**
2	Rocky	67	58	84	75	284
3	Ronald	67	98	78	69	312
4	Rumy	86	60	89	81	316
5	Bells	64	87	76	64	291
6	Sunny	78	60	89	73	300

Sample data

For example, in the above table:

1. To apply gray shading to the **Total** column only if the total marks scored by the student is greater than 300 and blue shading for the rest of the total.

   To apply Conditional Format, follow the steps given below:

   1. Create a new worksheet and enter the data as shown above.
   2. Select the cell range from F2:F6.
   3. Select **Conditional Formatting** from **Format** menu.
   4. A Conditional Formatting dialog box as shown below will be displayed.

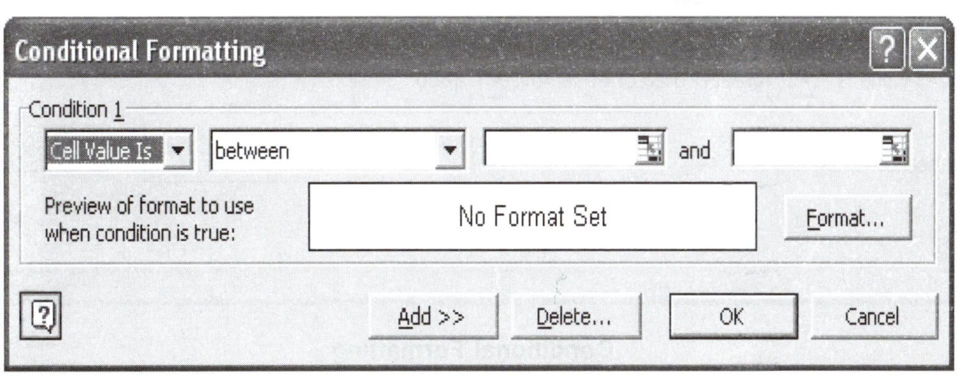

Conditional Formatting

5. Select 'greater than or equal to' function from the select drop-down list and type 300 in the right text box.

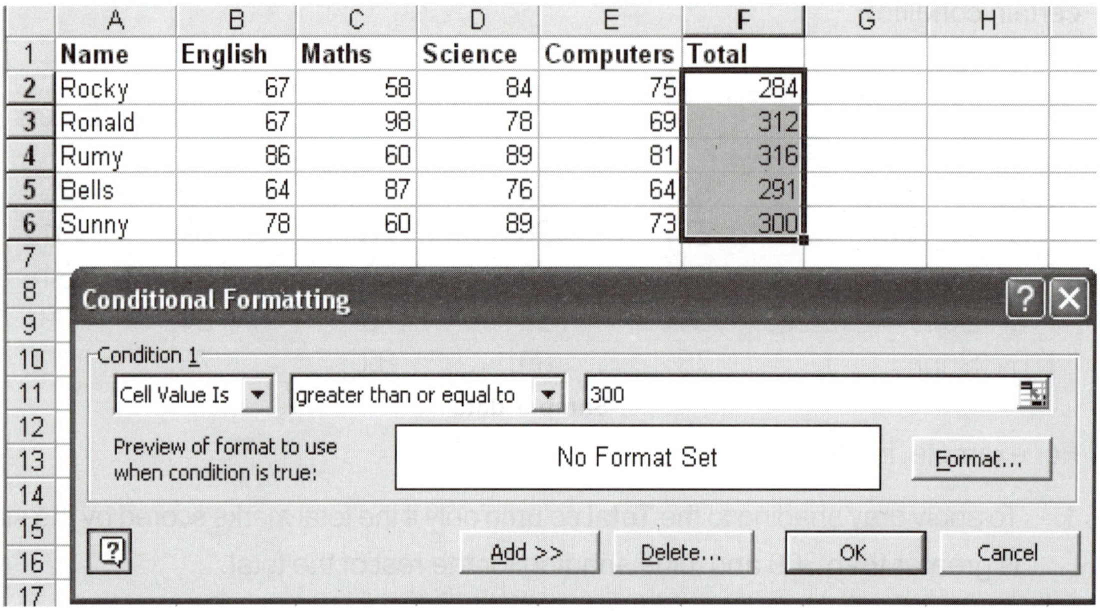

Conditional Formatting

6. Click on the **'Format'** button. The **'Format Cells'** dialog box appears.
7. Select 'Bold' and select grey from the colour box.
8. Click on OK button to close this dialog box. This will return you to the conditional formatting dialog box.

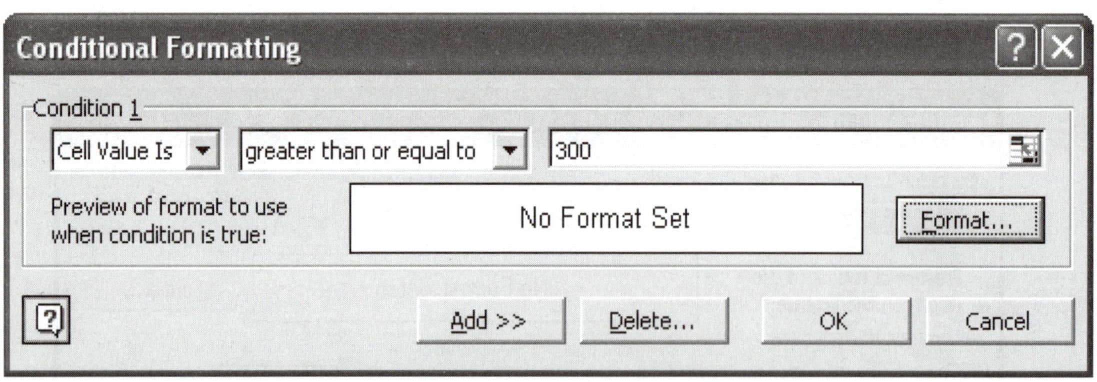

Conditional Formatting

The following table summarises the Conditional Formats applied to the cell as per the above example.

	Cell Value Is	Formula	Format
Condition 1	Greater than	300	Bold, Font colour gray

9. Then click on the **OK** button to close this dialog box.
10. The output will look like this.

	A	B	C	D	E	F
1	**Name**	**English**	**Maths**	**Science**	**Computers**	**Total**
2	Rocky	67	58	84	75	284
3	Ronald	67	98	78	69	**312**
4	Rumy	86	60	89	81	**316**
5	Bells	64	87	76	64	291
6	Sunny	78	60	89	73	**300**

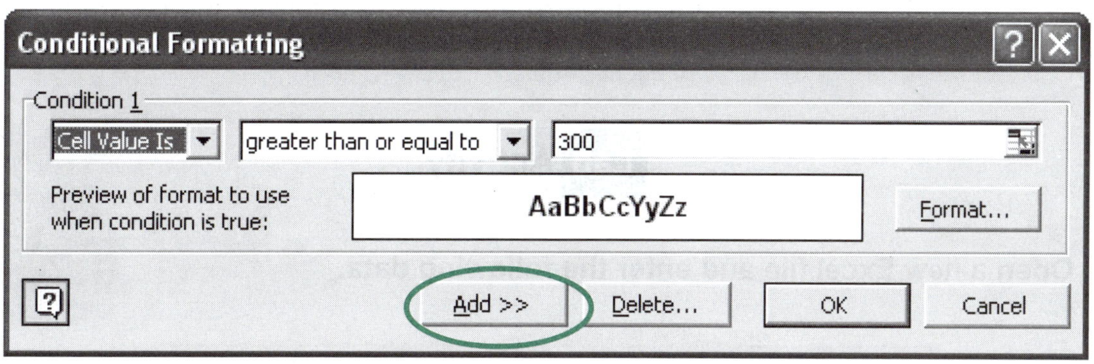

Conditional Formatting

The format of the cell will change once the value in it changes.

NOTE: If you want to add another condition, click **Add** and then repeat the Steps 5 to 9.

Summary

- AutoFormat automatically formats the data in a desired presentable form.
- Conditional Formatting is a feature that allows you to format the data that satisfies certain condition(s).

Exercises

1. Answer the following questions.

a. Define AutoFormat.

b. Define Conditional Formatting. Write the steps to apply Conditional Formatting?

2. Fill in the blanks.

a. The AutoFormat option is present in the ____________ menu.

b. The ____________ option automatically formats the data in a desired presentable form.

c. ____________________ is a feature that allows to format the data that satisfies certain condition.

Lab Activity

I. Open a new Excel file and enter the following data.

	A	B	C	D	E
1	Sl. No.	PRINCIPAL AMOUNT in Rs.	TIME TAKEN in yrs	RATE OF INTEREST in %age	SIMPLE INTEREST in Rs.
2	1	4600	2.0	2.0	
3	2	3400	1.3	2.0	
4	3	5600	3.0	3.0	
5	4	5300	2.2	2.5	
6	5	2900	2.6	3.5	
7	6	7800	1.4	3.0	

1. Calculate the simple interest for the above table.
2. Apply the conditional formatting for the simple interest column based on the following criteria to the cells.
    a. If simple interest is greater than 500 then,
       Font colour = red
       Font style = bold italics
    b. If simple interest is lesser than 300 then,
       Font colour = green
       Font style = italics
    c. Save this file in your folder under the file name 'principal.xls'

II. Enter the following data in a new Excel file and perform the operations that are given below.

	A	B	C	D	E	F	G	H
1	Name	English	Maths	Science	Social	Computers	Total	Average
2	Richard	77	51	33	78	77		
3	John	80	35	45	90	55		
4	Ronald	66	85	65	95	66		
5	Ben	55	66	87	94	65		

1. Find the Total of all the students.
2. Find the Average of all the students.
3. Apply conditional formatting for the above table using the following criteria.
    a. Students who have scored less than 35 in computer subject should be highlighted with RED colour.
    b. Students who have scored above 90 in maths should be highlighted in VIOLET.
    c. Students who have scored a total of 300 should be highlighted in GREEN.
    d. Students average more than 75% should be in bold and in YELLOW.
    e. English marks between 60 and 75 should be underlined with font style italics.

Trivia

Keyboarding Tips and Rules

1. Use the correct finger to strike each key.
2. Do not look at your hands while typing.
3. Sit up straight and feet flat on the floor.
4. Keep home row fingers touching home row keys even in a difficult reach.
5. It is also important to strike the keys with a short quick stroke.

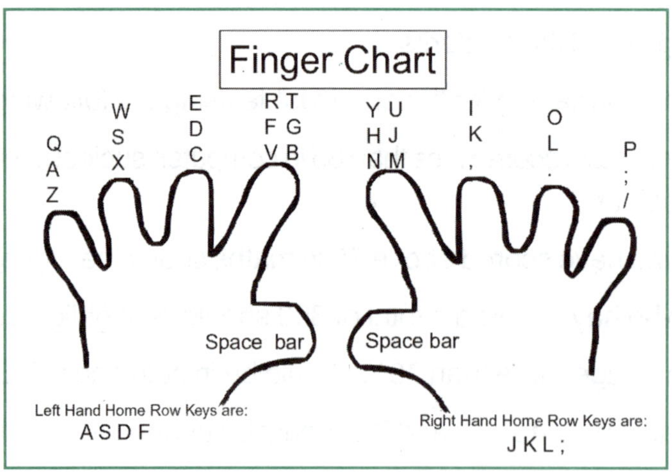

BACKGROUND AND SLIDE LAYOUT

Chapter 5

POWERPOINT-II

- **Changing the layout of a slide**
- **Changing the background colour**
- **Applying a shaded background**
- **Applying design template**

Learning Objective

To learn to apply background colour and layouts to the slides.

PowerPoint allows you to change the background and layout of the slides by changing the colour, shading, pattern, etc. You can also apply different design templates to the slides.

Changing the layout of a slide

You can easily change the slide layout from one format to another. For example, if you want to change from title slide to bulleted list then follow the steps given below:

1. Click on the **Format** menu and select **Slide Layout** option.

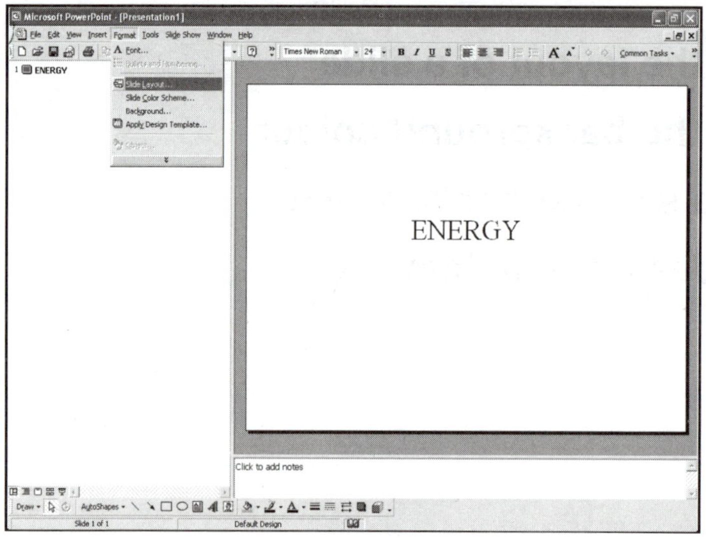

Slide Layout

2. The **Slide Layout** dialog box appears on the screen.
3. Choose the **'Bulleted List'** layout from the dialog box.

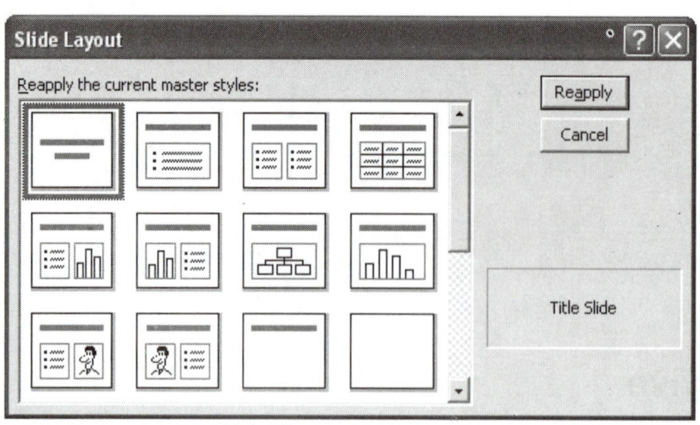

Slide Layout

4. Click on **Reapply** button.

Changing the Background colour

The BG colour and pattern can be applied to individual slide or same colour for all the slide.

1. Click on the **Format** menu and choose **Background** option.

   The **Background** dialog box will appear.

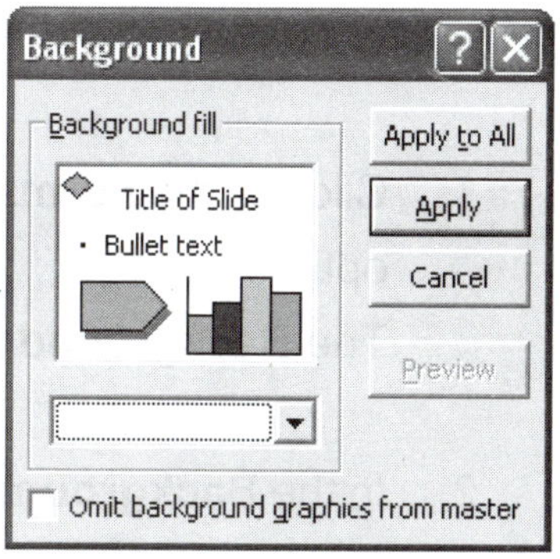

Background dialog box

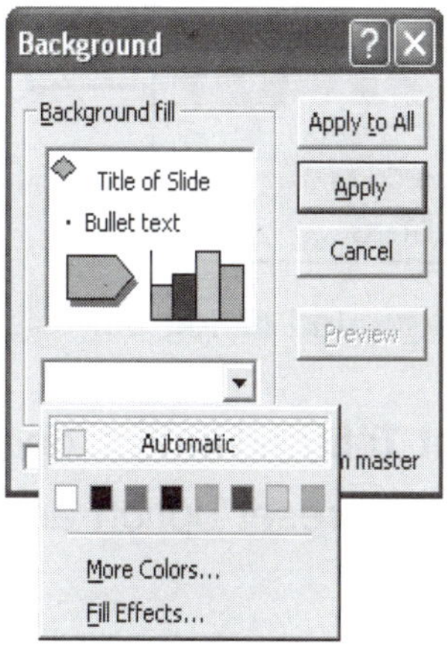

Background colour

2. Click on the down arrow in the **Background Fill** option.
3. Select the colour from the colour box to apply it as a background colour.
4. If you want more colours then click on **More Colors** option to display the **Colors** dialog box as shown.
5. Select a colour by clicking on it and then click on **OK** button.
6. The selected colour will be applied as the background.

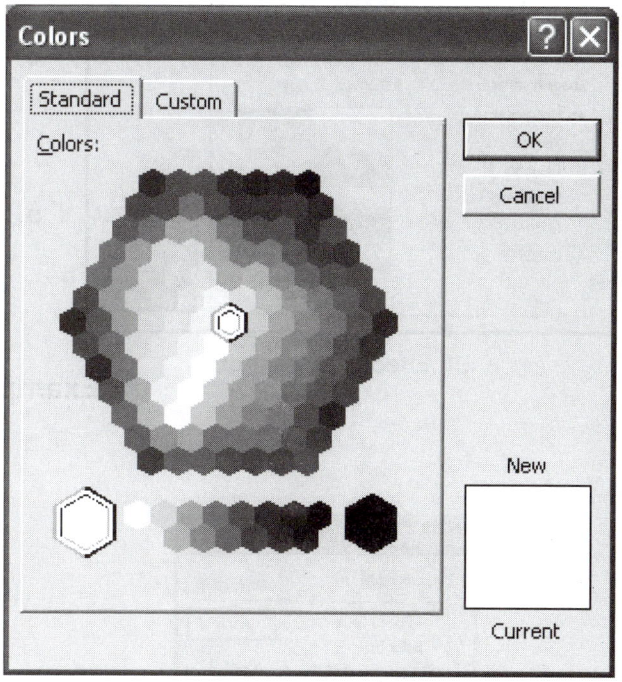

Colors dialog box

Applying a Shaded Background

1. Click on the **Format** menu and choose **Background** option.
   The **Background** dialog box will display as shown.

2. In the **Background Fill** box, click on the down arrow and then click on **Fill Effects**.
   The **Fill Effects** dialog box is displayed.

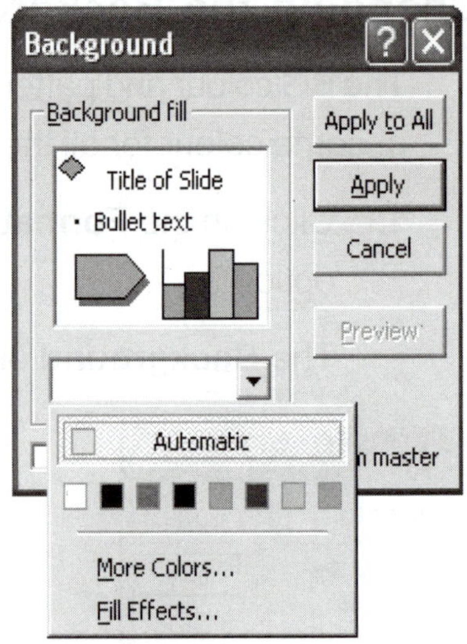

Background dialog box

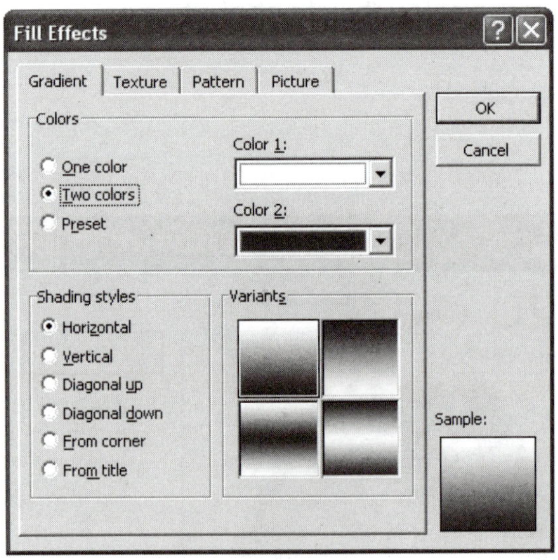

Fill Effects dialog box

3. Click on the **Gradient Tab** and select one colour or two colour or preset option and finally click on OK .
4. The **Background** dialog box is displayed with the shaded colours that you have chosen.
5. Click on **Apply** button to apply the changes to the current slide OR click on **Apply to All** button to apply changes to all the slides.

Example:

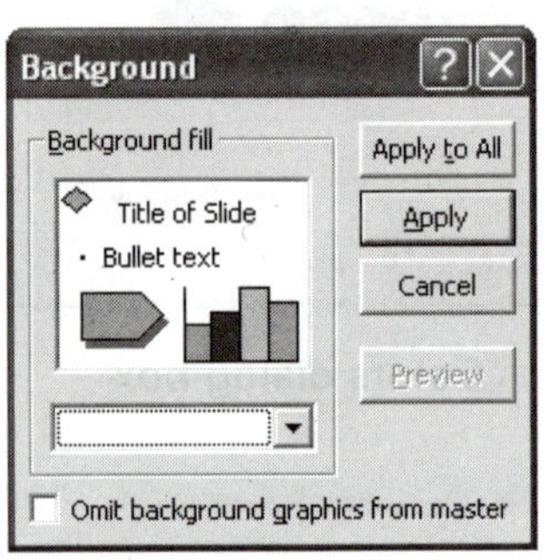

Background

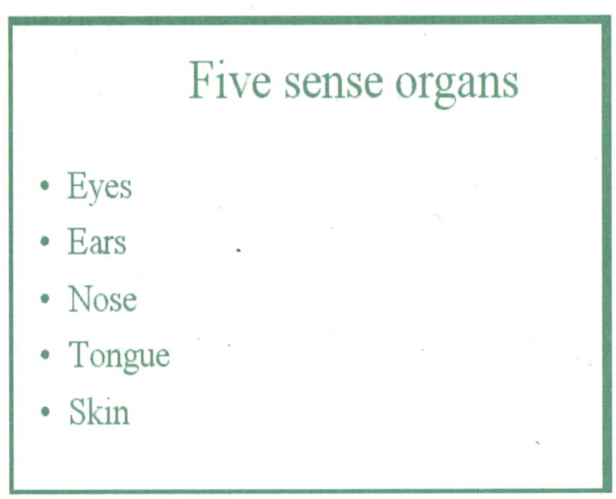

Applying Design Templates

Design Templates are pre-defined background formats, which will be applied to all the slides in the presentation.

To apply the design templates:

1. Click on **Format** menu and choose **Apply Design Template** option.

   The **Apply Design Template** dialog box is displayed as shown.

2. Select the design you want from the **'Look In'** dialog box. You can see the preview on the right side of the dialog box.

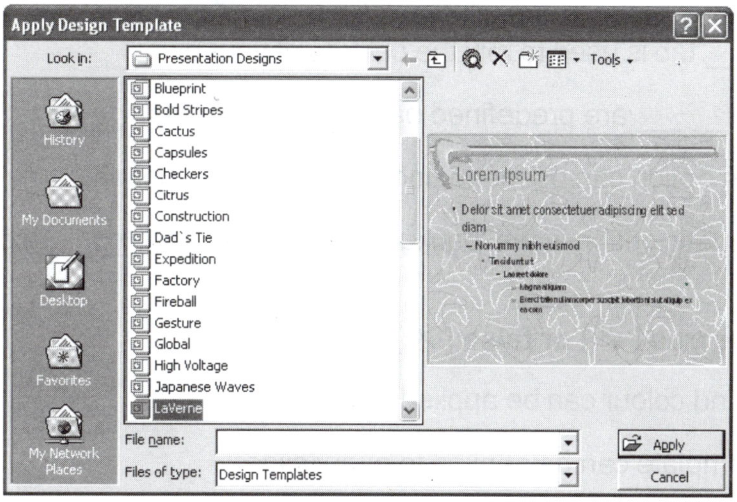

Apply Design Template

3. Click on **OK** button to apply the design to the presentations.

NOTE: In fill effects, you can apply a patterned or textured background to your slide in the same way as gradient tab.

Summary

- PowerPoint allows you to change the background and layout of the slides by changing the colour, shading, pattern, etc.
- Design Templates are pre-defined background formats, which will be applied to all the slides in the presentation.

Exercises

1. Answer the following questions.

a. How do you apply background colours to a slide?

b. How do you apply the shaded backgrounds using fill effects?

2. Fill in the blanks.

a. The __________ button is used to apply the changes to all slides.

b. __________ tab is used to mix the colours of your own.

c. __________ are predefined background formats.

d. Fill effects option can be found under __________ option.

e. The automatic option in the 'background fill' box has __________ colours.

3. State whether true [✔] or false [✕].

a. Background colour can be applied to every slide.

b. Design template can be applied to every slide.

c. You cannot apply shading to the presentation.

d. Slide layout option is used for inserting new slides.

e. Slide scheme option is used to change the slide layout.

4. Match the following.

a. To change the slide layout	i. Format → Background
b. To change the background colour	ii. Format → Apply Design Template
c. To apply design template	iii. Format → Slide Layout

Lab Activity

I. Design a presentation using the following data.

> **Respiratory system**
>
> All the cells in our body require energy to carry out diverse functions. The energy comes from the food we eat. Body cells absorb the digested food and use oxygen to release energy from it. The process of releasing energy from food is called respiration. Carbon dioxide and water vapour are formed as by-products during the process of respiration, which is a chemical process.
>
> Respiration is often confused with breathing. Breathing is the process of taking in oxygen-rich air from the environment and giving out carbon dioxide. Breathing is a purely physical process. The organs which are involved in the breathing process are called breathing or respiratory organs.
>
> The human respiratory system is made up of the following organs:
>
> 1. Nose: The nose encloses a nasal cavity which opens to the outside through two nostrils. Air enters the respiratory system through nose or mouth.
> 2. Larynx: Larynx or the voice-box is also called 'adam's apple' and is more prominent in men than in women.
> 3. Windpipe or Trachea: Trachea or the windpipe is a long, wide tube running through the neck in front of the oesophagus.
> 4. Bronchi: The trachea divides into two bronchi – each of which enters the lung on its own side.
> 5. Lungs: Lungs are like two elastic and conical bags. They are soft and spongy. This is because they contain lots of air.

1. Change the layout of the slide.
2. Apply a design template.
3. Apply a shaded background.

Trivia

Computer Processing Speed

Computer processing speed depends on a variety of factors. Three of the most important factors are:

- Word length (the number of bits that can be processed at one time by the microprocessor.)
- Cycle Speed (how fast individual events are processed, measured in Megahertz.)
- Data Bus Width (determines how much data can be transferred between the CPU and memory.)

Other factors Include:

- RAM (amount of available random access memory.)
- Disk Access Speed (speed that data can be read from hard disk.)
- Code Efficiency (how efficiently the computer code has been designed.)

Chapter 6

POWERPOINT-II

WORKING WITH GRAPHICS

- **Inserting ClipArt**
- **Inserting WordArt**
- **Inserting AutoShapes**
- **Creating an Organisation chart**
- **Grouping and Ungrouping**

Learning Objective

To learn to insert ClipArt, WordArt and AutoShapes

Microsoft PowerPoint provides two basic types of graphics to enhance presentations:

1. Drawing objects
2. Pictures

Drawing object includes AutoShapes, curves, lines freeform and WordArt.

Inserting a ClipArt, WordArt and AutoShapes

Inserting ClipArt

The ClipArt gallery provides a variety of pictures, photographs, sounds and videos that can be inserted in the presentations. The drawing toolbar can be used to add and also draw objects in the presentation.

To insert a picture from the ClipArt gallery into a slide, follow the steps given below:

1. Click on the **Insert** menu.
2. Select **Picture** option and select **ClipArt.**

OR

Click on **ClipArt button**  from the drawing toolbar.

The **Insert ClipArt** dialog box is displayed as shown below.

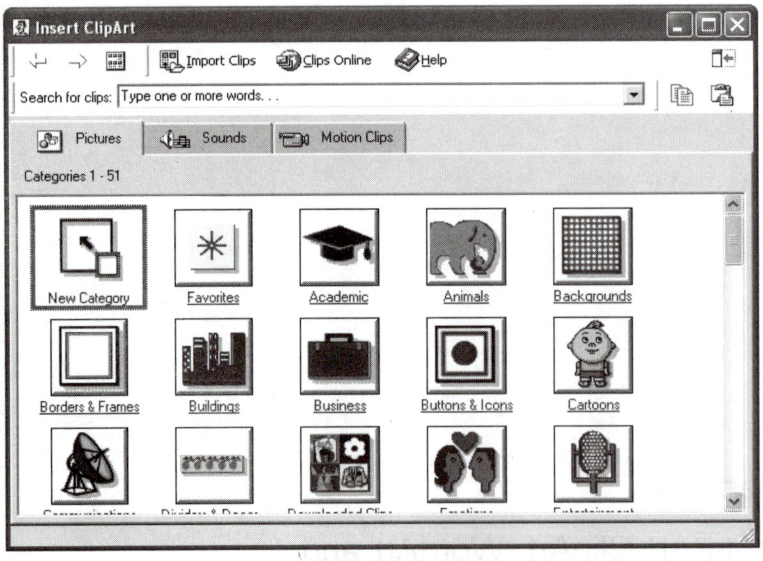

Insert ClipArt dialog box

3. Select the category you want.
4. Click on the picture you want to insert.
5. Click on the **Insert Clip** option.

Insert ClipArt

The inserted ClipArt will be placed in the slide.

ClipArt

NOTE: You can resize the object.

Inserting WordArt

The artistic text can be created using WordArt on the drawing toolbar.

The text can be shadowed, skewed, rotated or stretched to make the text effective.

For inserting WordArt, follow the steps as follows:

1. Click on **WordArt** symbol  on the drawing toolbar.
2. WordArt dialog box is displayed. Type the text you want to display.
3. Click on OK button. WordArt will be inserted in the current slide.

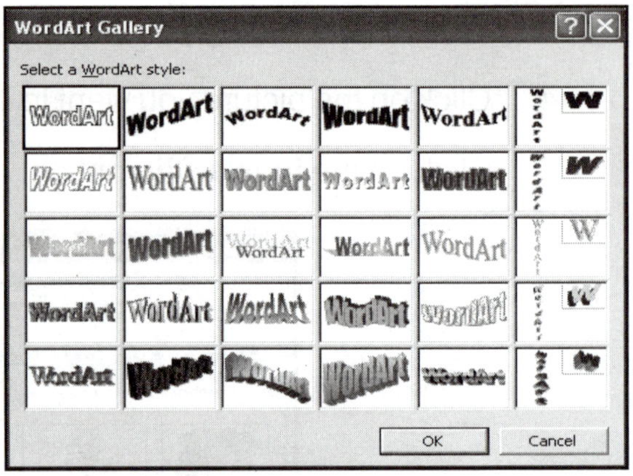

WordArt

Inserting AutoShapes

The AutoShape allows us to draw different geometrical shapes like arrows, flowchart symbols, stars and banners on the document. PowerPoint provides a set of ready-made AutoShapes that you can use in your presentations. Using these AutoShapes you can resize, rotate flip, colour and combine the shapes. The AutoShapes include several categories of Shapes, Lines, Basic shapes, Flowchart elements, Stars and Banners and Callouts. Using these you can draw a freeform drawing.

To insert AutoShapes

1. Click on the **AutoShapes**  button on the drawing toolbar.
2. Point to the category you want and select the shape you want.

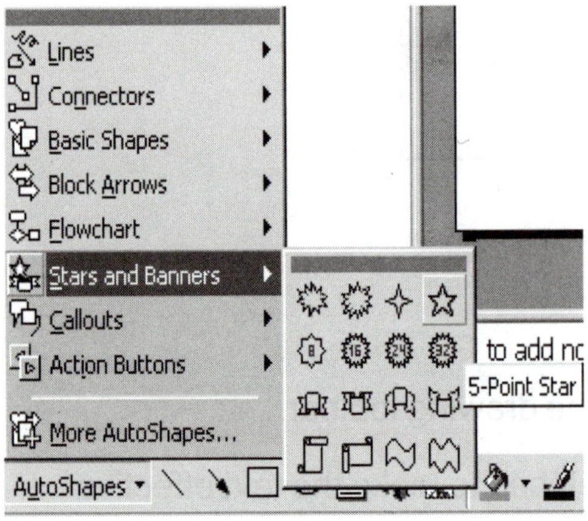

AutoShapes

AutoShapes inserted

Creating an Organisation Chart

Organisation chart is used to graphically display hierarchal relationships.

1. Click on **File** menu and select **New** option.
2. The **New Slide** layout dialog box appears.
3. Choose the **Organisation Chart** layout.
4. Type the title that you want on the title slide.
5. Double-click the organisation chart to open the Microsoft Organisation Chart.
6. Enter the contents to the organisation chart using tools and menus.

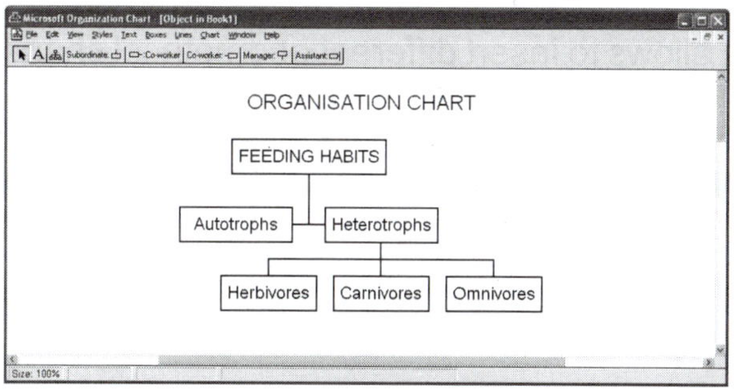

Organisation Chart

7. Click **File** → **Exit,** to return to the PowerPoint.

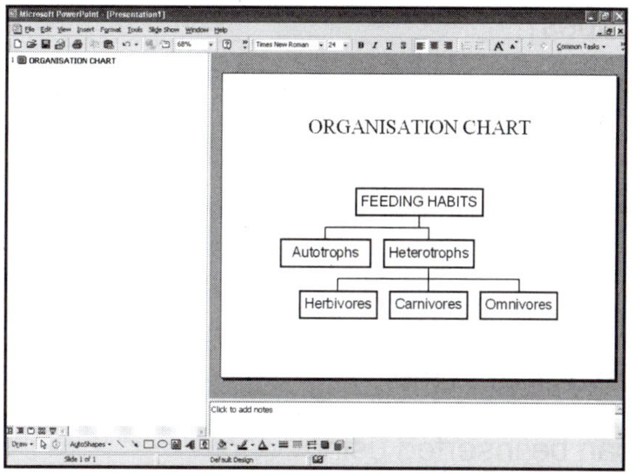

Organisation Chart

Grouping and Ungrouping

Grouping is used to combine different objects into one which helps in moving or copying them to a different location or to resize the objects together. Ungrouping is used to split the grouped objects.

To group the objects select the object which you wish to group and right click, a context menu will appear, select group option.

To ungroup the objects right click on the object, a context menu will appear, select ungroup option.

Summary

- The ClipArt gallery provides a variety of pictures, photographs, sounds and videos that can be inserted into the presentation.
- WordArt is used to create artistic text.
- The AutoShape allows to insert different geometrical shapes.
- Organisation chart is used to graphically display hierarchal relationships.

Exercises

1. Answer the following questions.

a. What are ClipArts?

b. What are AutoShapes?

c. Write the steps for inserting AutoShapes.

d. What is WordArt?

e. State the difference between ClipArt and WordArt.

2. Fill in the blanks.

a. ClipArt option is available in the insert menu.

b. Decorative text can be inserted using wordart.

c. The autoshape option allows to insert different geometrical shapes.

d. The AutoShape button is present on the drawing toolbar.

3. Match the following.

A	B
a. 	i. AutoShape button
b. 	ii. To draw a square or rectangle
c. 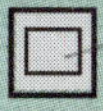	iii. To insert decorative text
d. 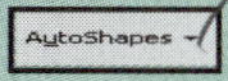	iv. To insert ClipArts

4. Crossword

Clues:

Across

1. It allows us to add images to the document
2. Displays the different design patterns of the slides
3. They are pre-defined back ground formats

Down

4. Shapes that can be inserted automatically without drawing
5. Used to create decorative text
6. The fill effect option can be found under this

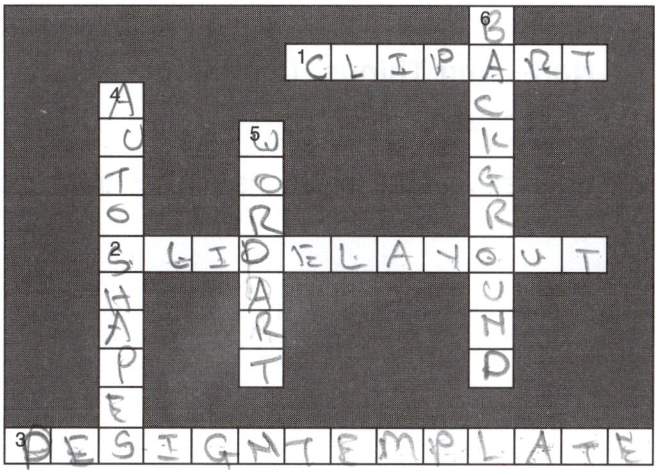

Lab Activity

I. Create a presentation on the topic "Balance in Nature" with minimum of 10 slides, which have different background colours.

II. Create a presentation on the topic "Our Environment".

1. Insert 3–4 slide in the presentation.
2. Apply design templates for the slides.

3. Use necessary graphics for the content.
4. Use decorative text for the topic headings.

Use all formatting tools you have learned to make the presentation attractive.

III. Create a presentation on the topic **"The world of living organism"**.

1. Apply design templates for the slides.
2. Give different font colours to the contents.
3. Use necessary graphics.
4. Use decorative text for the topic headings.

IV. Create a presentation with background shadings applied for 5 slides on **Living and Non-living Things.** Use the necessary graphics and AutoShapes to make the presentation.

V. Save all your presentations in a separate folder.

SIDE STRETCH

Clasp hands together above head with palms upward; slowly lean to the right, then to the left, keep knees slightly bent; do not arch back; repeat three times.

Chapter

7

NETWORK-II

TYPES OF NETWORK

- **Types of Network**
- **Components of LAN**
- **Server and its types**
- **LAN cables**

Learning Objective

To learn about different types of networks and LAN components.

Types of Network

The three basic types of networks include:

LAN (Local Area Network)

MAN (Metropolitan Area Network)

WAN (Wide Area Network)

Local Area Network (LAN)

A LAN is a connection of computers confined relatively to a small area. It is generally limited to a building or a geographical area, of not more than a mile.

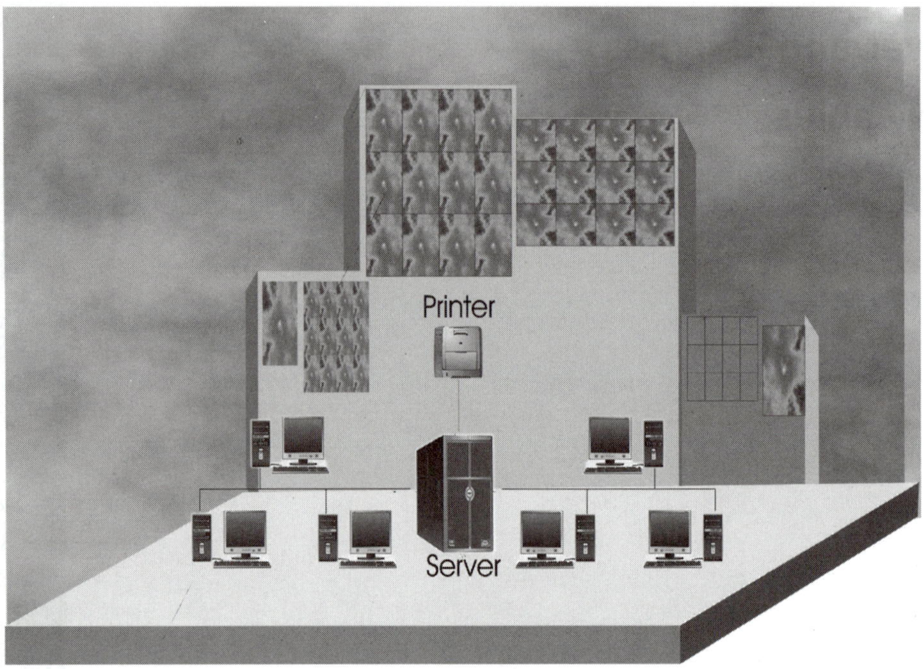

Local Area Network

Metropolitan Area Network (MAN)

MAN covers larger geographic areas, such as cities. Often, these types of networks are used by local libraries and government agencies to connect to citizens and also to private industries.

Wide Area Network (WAN)

WAN connects large geographic areas, like one country to another country. In this type of network, dedicated transoceanic cabling or satellite uplinks may be used.

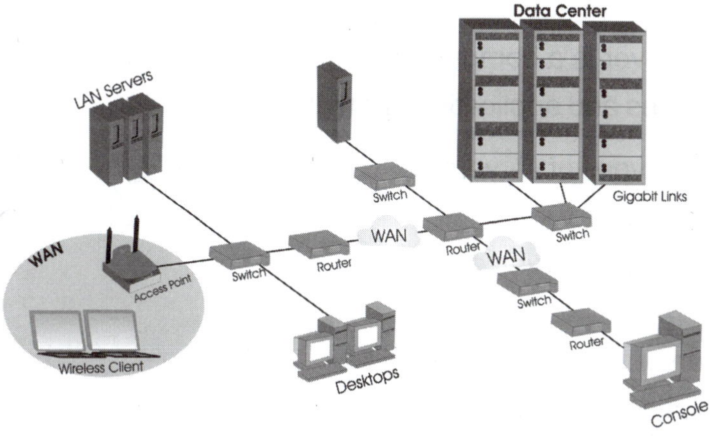

Wide Area Network

Components of LAN

The LAN configuration consists of:

- Workstation
- Server

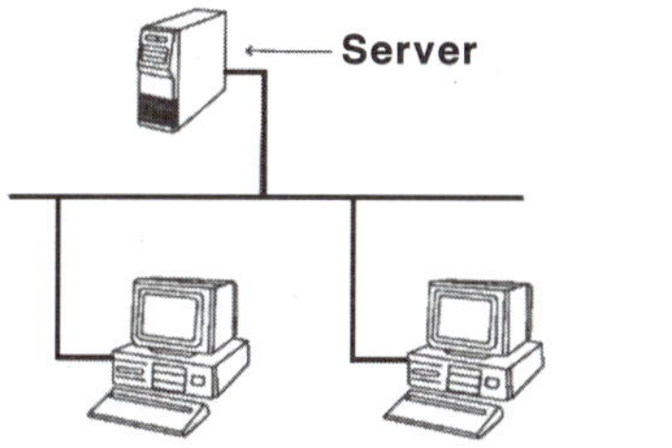

Components of LAN

Workstation

The Workstation is a computer connected to the server where input and output operations are carried out.

Server

Server is a computer that provides services to a workstation. The various services are:

1. Processing
2. Storage
3. Sharing of files, resources, etc.
4. Management of workstations and servers

Types of Servers

We know that a server is a computer that serves the workstation. All the workstations access the data, files and applications from the server.

There are different types of servers:

- Dedicated server
- Non-dedicated server
- File server
- Print server
- Communication server

Dedicated Server

In most LANs, the only job of the server is to help the workstation in accessing the data, files, software and hardware resources. The server is dedicated only for handling huge workloads. Such a server is called dedicated server.

Non-Dedicated Server

The server is also one of the workstations in some LAN. The server acts as a workstation and also as a server. Such a server is called non-dedicated server.

File Server

The file server is a computer that holds the file for the client computers. Server must be a high-quality, heavy-duty machine, because it serves the whole network. A file server stands at the heart of most networks. It is a very fast computer with a large amount of RAM and storage space, along with a fast network interface card.

The file server controls the communication of information between the nodes on a network. For example, it may be asked to send a word processor program to one workstation, receive a database file from another workstation, and store an e-mail message during the same time period. This requires a computer that can store a lot of information and share it very quickly.

Print Server

Print server is special software that is executed by a computer to make the printer available for sharing across the network. The client systems request the print jobs to print server. The print server queues the job and sends them to the printer in an order.

Communication Server

Communication server or access server helps you to dial into network and run application program.

LAN Cables

LAN cables are the connecting cables or communication channels. These cables play a major role in a network to provide maximum protection, quality of transfer of data and good performance.

Cable is the medium through which information usually moves from one network device to another. There are several types of cables, which are commonly used with LANs. They are:

- Unshielded Twisted Pair (UTP) Cables
- Shielded Twisted Pair (STP) Cables
- Coaxial Cable
- Fibre Optic Cable

More details on these cables will be provided in the next level.

Summary

- LAN is a small area network.
- MAN covers larger geographic areas, such as cities.
- WAN connects larger geographic areas such as countries.
- Server is a computer that stores all the software that controls the network, as well as the software that can be shared by the computers attached to the network.
- The workstation is a computer connected to the server.
- Types of server:
  - Dedicated server
  - Non-dedicated server
  - File server
  - Print server
  - Communication server

Exercises

1. Answer the following questions.

a. Define LAN.

b. Define MAN.

c. Define WAN.

d. Explain the components of LAN.

2. Fill in the blanks.

a. ____________ is a computer connected to the server.

b. The ____________ server is a computer that holds the file for the client computers.

c. ____________ is a small area network.

d. __________ connects larger geographic areas such as countries.

3. State whether true [✔] or false [✕].

a. Server is a computer that provides services to a workstation.

b. LAN covers large geographic areas, such as countries.

c. LAN cables are the connecting cables or communication channels.

4. Multiple choice questions.

a. The connection of computers confined to a small area is called__________.

i. LAN	ii. MAN
iii. WAN	iv. None of the above

b. The connection of computers that covers larger geographical areas such as cities are called__________.

i. LAN	ii. WAN
iii. MAN	iv. None of the above

Project

1. Create a document on the topic "Our Environment" using Microsoft Word and perform the following operations.

a. Make use of bulleted and numbered lists.

b. Make use of table properties to give information about the biotic and abiotic components.

c. Make use of AutoFormat feature.

d. Apply borders and shading to the table.

e. Move the tables to the center of the screen.

f. Center align the text and make the column headings bold.

g. Resize the table.

h. Find the total number of biotic components using formula in tables.

i. Add ClipArt related to the environment.

j. Add an image from the file and use edit option.

k. Insert AutoShapes in your document.

l. Insert WordArt to give an artistic look to your document.

2. Create a Spreadsheet of marks scored by the students in your class in the annual exam and perform the following operations.

a. Find the total of few students.

b. Find the total of remaining students using AutoSum feature.

c. Find the average of all the subjects in the average column.

d. Count the number of students in the class.

e. Find the maximum marks scored by the student.

f. Find the minimum marks scored by the student.

g. Apply the conditional formatting for the above table using the following criteria:

   i. The names of students who have scored less than 35 in maths should be highlighted in Red.

ii. The names of students who have scored above 90 in science should be highlighted in Green.

iii. The names of students who have scored a total of 300 should be highlighted in Pink.

iv. The names of students with an average of more than 80% should be in Bold and Yellow.

h. Display the " Result" as "Pass" if the student has scored marks>=35 in each subject otherwise as "Fail". Display the class score according to the conditions given below:

i. If average >=30 and average < 50 then "Third class"

ii. If average >= 50 and average <60 then "Second class"

iii. If average >=60 and average < 80 then "First class"

iv. If average >= 80 then "Distinction" Otherwise display "Null"

3. Create a presentation on the topic "Energy" and perform the following operations.

a. Insert a minimum of 4–5 slides in the presentation.

b. Change the layout of the slide and observe the difference.

c. Apply a design template for the slides.

d. Apply a shaded background.

e. Make use of all the formatting tools.

f. Insert ClipArt that are relevant to the topic.

g. Insert AutoShapes.

h. Create decorative text using WordArt.

i. Give different font colour to the contents.

Computer Vocabulary

Table: A collection of rows and columns.

Row: In excel it is the horizontal lines of the cells.

Column: In excel it is the vertical lines of the cells.

Borders: It is used to highlight important information.

Bulleted lists: Displays various patterns of bullets.

Numbered list: Displays various patterns of numbers.

Graphics: Designs that give impressive look to the document.

Editing: Means making changes to the existing document.

WordArt: It is used to create decorative text.

ClipArt: It is used to add images to the document.

AutoShapes: Shapes that can be inserted automatically without drawing.

Functions: Pre-defined formula for performing a particular task.

Sum: Function used to add the numbers.

AutoSum: Function that automatically calculates the sum of numbers.

Maximum: It finds the largest value from a given set of numbers.

Minimum: It finds the smallest value from a given set of numbers.

Count: This function counts the number of selected cells that contain data.

AutoFormat: Automatically formats the data in a desired presentable form.

Shaded background: It applies colour background.

Slide layout: It is used to view the different design patterns of the slides.

Design template: They are the pre-defined background format.

Conditional format: They are used for formatting data based on conditions.

Presentation: A systematic display of information.

Technology

Flash drives

USB Drives are consistently gaining popularity. They are an extremely simple, safe and affordable method of removable file storage. USB Drives are also sometimes called as Pen Drive, USB Flash Drive, Thumb Drive or Jump Drive. They are offered in many shapes and file storage capacities.

USB drives have several advantages over the other portable storage devices, particularly the floppy disk. They are generally faster, hold more data, and are considered more reliable than floppy disks. The storage sizes offered range from 32 MB to 4 GB.

The USB Drive is compatible with Windows ME / Windows XP / Windows 2000 / Mac 8.6 or above / Linux 2.4.0 or above, without the use of any device driver.

To use a USB Drive could not be more easier. All you need to do is to plug it into an open USB port and it will be automatically identified by your computer system and will quickly become available for use. It will now appear in "My Computer" as a new Removable Disk, and as signed the next available drive letter. You use the USB Drive just like you would use your Floppy Drive. Send files to it, or drag and drop them in it.

Safe removal of your USB Drive:

When you are ready to remove your USB Flash Drive, it is advisable that you follow the safe removal method recommended by Windows. This is to ensure that you are not removing the drive while it is still in use. The procedure is as follows:

In the taskbar at the bottom right of your screen, you will find the **Safely Remove Hardware** icon.

Double click the **Safely Remove Hardware** icon and from the resulting window.

Select the device that you want to unplug or eject from the **Hardware devices** menu, then click on **Stop**. When Windows notifies you that it is safe to do so, unplug the device from your computer.

IT Personality

Mr. Robert Metcalfe

(Inventor of Ethernet)

Background

- Robert Metcalfe was born in Brooklyn, New York in 1946.
- He graduated from the Massachusetts Institute of Technology in 1969 with B.S. degrees one in Electrical Engineering and the other in management.
- In 1970, he received his M.S. degree and in 1973, he completed his PhD in Applied Mathematics from Harvard University.

Achievements and Awards

- His doctoral dissertation, 'Packet Communication', was about the early Internet.
- The next eight years, Metcalfe worked at the Xerox Palo Alto Research Center.
- He invented Ethernet, the local computer-networking standard that today connects over 100 million computers to the Internet.
- In 1979, Metcalfe founded **3Com** Corporation, the $6-billion computer-networking company, where he was at various times chairman, president and CEO. He retired from **3Com** in 1990.
- In 1988, he received the **Alexander Graham Bell** Medal from the Institute of Electrical and Electronics Engineers (IEEE).
- Metcalfe received the **National Medal of Technology** from President Bush in a White House ceremony on March 14, 2005, "for leadership in the invention, standardisation, and commercialisation of Ethernet."

IT Personality

Mr. Christian Huitema
(Communication protocol)

Background

- Christian Huitema was born in France on 13 January 1953.
- He studied at the Ecole Polytechnique in Paris from 1972 to 1975.
- In 1985, he obtained a Doctorate in Sciences from the University Pierre at Marie Curie.

Achievements and Awards

- Between 1975 and 1980, he worked as a software engineer at SEMA, first porting large Fortran programs to new architecture and then developed large Cobol applications for manufacture control.
- From 1980 to 1985, he worked at CNET (Centre National d'Etudes des Telecommunications).
- He then worked on a joined project between CNET and INRIA, where he developed communication protocols for the SM90 workstation.
- He has conducted research on various areas of computer networking, such as satellite communication, transport protocols, marshaling languages and compilers, mail and name services.
- Huitema was a member of the Internet Architecture Board (IAB) from 1991 to 1996. He was elected a trustee of the Internet Society in May 1995.
- Huitema has written a fairly large number of scientific publications, articles and conference communications, as well as three books.
- Christian Huitema joined Microsoft in February 2000, as "Architect" in the "Windows Networking and Communications" group.

NOTES

NOTES